INDEPENDENCE
IN AFRICA

CAUSES AND CONSEQUENCES

World War I
The Great Depression
World War II
Independence in Africa
The African American Civil Rights Movement
The Arab-Israeli Conflict
The Rise of Japan and the Pacific Rim
The Vietnam War
The Collapse of Communism in Eastern Europe
The End of Apartheid

CAUSES AND CONSEQUENCES

OF

INDEPENDENCE IN AFRICA

KEVIN SHILLINGTON

RSVP

**RAINTREE
STECK-VAUGHN**
P U B L I S H E R S
The Steck-Vaughn Company

Austin, Texas

Published by Raintree Steck-Vaughn Publishers, an imprint of Steck-Vaughn Company

Developed by the Creative Publishing Company
Editor: Helena Ramsay
Designed by Ian Winton

Raintree Steck-Vaughn Publishers staff
Project Manager: Lyda Guz
Editors: Shirley Shalit, Pam Wells
Electronic Production: Scott Melcer
Consultants: Patricia Romero, Towson State University
Michael M. Morrogh, Shrewsbury School

Cover photo (large): Young people celebrate Namibia's independence from South Africa in Windhoek, 1990. March 21 was chosen in memory of those who died in the Sharpeville massacre in 1960.
Cover photo (small): In 1910, the last African rebels in Ivory Coast finally submit to European, in this case French, control.

Library of Congress Cataloging-in-Publication Data

Shillington, Kevin.
    Causes and consequences of independence in Africa / Kevin Shillington.
       p.   cm. — (Causes and consequences)
    Includes bibliographical references (p. 76) and index.
    Summary: Examines the beginning of the independence movement in Africa and the results once freedom was achieved.
    ISBN 0-8172-4060-8
    1. Africa — Politics and government — 1945-1960 — Juvenile literature.   2. Africa — History — Autonomy and independence movements — Juvenile literature.   3. Africa — Politics and government — 1960- — Juvenile Literature.   4. Colonies — Africa — History — Juvenile literature.
[1. Africa — Politics and government — 1945-1960. 2. Africa — Politics and government — 1960-
3. Africa — History — Autonomy and independence movements.]
I. Title. II. Series.
DT29.S52   1998
960.3'2—dc21   97-29777
                                                 CIP AC

Printed in Hong Kong
Bound in the United States
1 2 3 4 5 6 7 8 9 0 LB 01 00 99 98 97

CONTENTS

INTRODUCTION

The common images of Africa, as portrayed on the television screens or in the magazines and newspapers of North America and Western Europe, fall into various categories. The most common view is that Africa is a land full of wild animals in game parks, with Africans playing merely a background role as gamekeepers or poachers. Alternative images bring Africans themselves to the front, but here they are seen either as backward, ill-educated, impoverished, and in need of Western aid, or as ill-trained soldiers involved in tribal warfare and the massacre of civilians. In either case, Africans are shown in a very unflattering light. The final category is the picture most often shown on television screens. It is of starving women and children in refugee camps. All of these images may be factually true, but they are only a fraction of the total picture. Shown in isolation like this, they portray a very distorted version of the reality that is Africa today.

One of the great achievements of independent Africa has been the spread of education throughout the continent. The smiling faces of these Ghanaian schoolchildren represent the future hopes of Africa.

A MODERN MAP

A point that fails to come across in any of the above images is that Africa is a huge continent, and one of great diversity. Second only to Asia in terms of size, Africa contains some 500 million people and covers an area of over 11.5 million square miles (30 million sq km). The Mediterranean climate of the north gives way to desert, savannah, tropical rain forest at the heart of the continent, and drier scrub lands in the south. In the southwestern Cape the climate is again Mediterranean.

Africa's people are very diverse, too. They are divided today into no fewer than 54 separate countries. Unlike most other parts of the world, the countries of Africa are very recent, largely artificial creations. Most of Africa's modern boundaries were drawn by Europeans at the end of the nineteenth century, with little or no regard for the realities of African nationality or politics, and almost entirely against the wishes of Africans themselves. How and why did this come about, and what have been its consequences?

TRADING WITH EUROPE

The seafaring nations of Western Europe — Portugal, the Netherlands, Britain, Denmark, and France — began to trade with the peoples of western Africa in the late fifteenth century. It started on a small scale, with Europeans buying African gold, ivory, and ebony in exchange for European cloths, metal goods, and beads. In the seventeenth and eighteenth centuries, however, most commerce between Africa and Europe was dominated by the notorious slave trade, as European merchants sought African slave labor to work the mines and plantations of the Caribbean and the Americas. Although the Atlantic slave trade was initiated and conducted by Europeans, African rulers and their agents also played a vital part in the traffic, waging war on their neighbors and sending their unfortunate captives to the coasts to be sold into slavery.

Gradually, opponents of the slave trade began to emerge, in Africa, the Americas, and Europe. By the late eighteenth century these voices were beginning to be heard. Thus, in the early nineteenth century, the slave trade was slowly abolished, and Europeans looked to Africa for other commodities to trade.

By this time the industrial revolution was transforming the economies of Western Europe, giving them technical superiority over many other peoples of the world. Throughout the nineteenth century the industrialists of Europe looked to Africa as a rich source of raw materials such as palm oil, ground nuts, and cotton, of valuable minerals like gold, copper, and tin, and of luxuries such as ivory, ebony, and ostrich feathers, which were used largely for decorating hats.

Moreover, Africa was seen as a huge market for European and American goods. Europe had already begun to export cloth and weapons to Africa during the eighteenth century. The trade that began as part of the slave trade continued and developed as part of export trade. As slavery was gradually abolished, this aspect of export trade developed very quickly. The trade from the United States in tobacco, building materials, wood for naval building, and weapons was brisk. British and French cotton manufacturers exported cheap cloth to Africa.

European merchants, backed up by their governments, competed with each other to monopolize the trade along the African coast, making treaties with

The slave trade continued in central Africa until the closure of the slave markets of Zanzibar (1873) and Brazil (1888). Here, a British artist records the transportation of captives through Angola for sale into slavery in 1873.

certain African rulers and using force to make others trade exclusively with them. The discovery of diamonds in South Africa in 1870 heightened European expectations. They believed that there was an enormous natural storehouse of untapped wealth in Africa.

Europeans grew impatient with the Africans' desire to keep control of the trade themselves. They complained of the way African rulers imposed taxes and restrictions on the exploitation of minerals and on the movement of goods in and out of their kingdoms. By the mid-1880s western European governments concluded that the only way to secure the African trade to their own advantage, was to take control of the continent itself. However, European rivalry and mistrust, which was to lead eventually to the outbreak of World War I in 1914, was already apparent in Africa in the 1880s.

THE SCRAMBLE FOR AFRICA

By the late nineteenth century Britain, France, and Germany had joined Belgium and Portugal in seizing colonies in Africa. This desperately competitive period became known as "the scramble for Africa." European forces were at an advantage in Africa. They had the military superiority of the latest modern weapons such as explosive shells and mobile machine-guns. In addition,

Kimberley diamond mine in British-controlled South Africa. This contemporary artist's view was published in the Illustrated London News *in 1872. Notice the artist's portrayal of the relationship between blacks and whites.*

We must hurry up . . . . Our rivals [the British and the Germans] are setting out from the coast for the interior. We must surprise them by our march on Chad.

The French explorer Savorgnan de Brazza, in a public speech in France, 1886, following his recent return from the Congo. Quoted in R. Hallett, Africa since 1875 *(Heinemann, London, 1974), page 443.*

The major wars of colonial conquest were over by 1900. However, it was not until 1910, as recorded here, that the last African rebels in Ivory Coast finally submitted to European control — in this case the French.

FIN DE LA RÉVOLTE DE LA COTE D'IVOIRE
Les Abbeys font leur soumission

We are the finest race in the world and . . . the more of the world we inhabit the better it is for the human race. Why should we not form a secret society with but one object, the furtherance of the British Empire and the bringing of the whole uncivilized world under British rule . . . . Africa is still lying ready for us (and) it is our duty to take it.

From Confession of Faith *by Cecil Rhodes, 1877.*

many of the more formidable African nations had been divided and weakened by centuries of the slave trade as well as internal disorder. Africans who resisted European invasion suffered brutal military conquest. Others, seeing what had happened to their neighbors, peacefully submitted to European control. In some places, there were even incidents of African collaboration with the colonial forces.

By the early 1900s Africa had been politically transformed. With the sole exceptions of Ethiopia and Liberia (which had strong ties to the United States) all the countries of Africa had been brought within the empires of western Europe. The colonial era had begun.

European colonial control of Africa was to last for little more than half a century. How was it that Europe, which had gained control of the continent so completely and so rapidly at the end of the nineteenth century, was to lose it so suddenly in the middle of the twentieth century? What were the causes of this complete turnaround? How, and why, did Africans gain their independence from European colonialism? What were the consequences of that independence for Africa? These are the questions which this book sets out to answer.

This map shows Africa at the outbreak of World War I in 1914. With the exception of Ethiopia and the tiny state of Liberia, every country was ruled by the imperial powers of Western Europe.

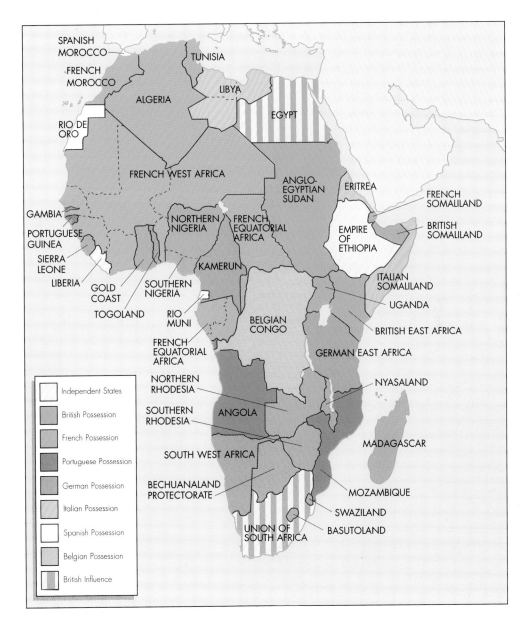

SPANISH MOROCCO
FRENCH MOROCCO
TUNISIA
LIBYA
ALGERIA
EGYPT
RIO DE ORO
FRENCH WEST AFRICA
ANGLO-EGYPTIAN SUDAN
ERITREA
FRENCH SOMALILAND
GAMBIA
NORTHERN NIGERIA
FRENCH EQUATORIAL AFRICA
EMPIRE OF ETHIOPIA
BRITISH SOMALILAND
PORTUGUESE GUINEA
SIERRA LEONE
LIBERIA
GOLD COAST
SOUTHERN NIGERIA
KAMERUN
ITALIAN SOMALILAND
TOGOLAND
RIO MUNI
BELGIAN CONGO
UGANDA
BRITISH EAST AFRICA
FRENCH EQUATORIAL AFRICA
GERMAN EAST AFRICA
NORTHERN RHODESIA
NYASALAND
SOUTHERN RHODESIA
ANGOLA
SOUTH WEST AFRICA
MADAGASCAR
BECHUANALAND PROTECTORATE
MOZAMBIQUE
SWAZILAND
UNION OF SOUTH AFRICA
BASUTOLAND

Independent States
British Possession
French Possession
Portuguese Possession
German Possession
Italian Possession
Spanish Possession
Belgian Possession
British Influence

THE COLONIAL ERA

Each imperial power developed its own "style" of rule in Africa. At times, the rule of one imperial power was better than that of another. The British, for example, had a certain respect for African customary law and did not regularly resort to forced labor like the French. Ultimately, however, from an African viewpoint, the similarities of colonial oppression were far more significant than the differences of style.

The "rise of African nationalism" is the phrase used to describe the development of the movement toward independence from colonial rule. The desire for independence reached its height in the 1950s and early 1960s. It was so powerful that between 1956 and 1966 no fewer than 33 African countries gained their independence from French, Belgian, or British rule.

The European rulers of Africa were caught by surprise — they had not anticipated such a strong desire in Africa for independence. Until 1950, they had assumed that they would still be ruling Africa for many decades to come. For Africans, however, the movement came as no surprise. The underlying desire for freedom from European control and interference had never been far from their minds. When one looks at the nature of colonialism from an African viewpoint, their motives are easily understood.

EUROPEAN INVASION

The memory of military conquest lived on in many African countries. In the 1940s, anyone over age 30 would have heard firsthand accounts of invasion by European soldiers during the scramble for Africa. Their parents — or grandparents — would have witnessed the fighting, or taken part in it themselves. In what is now Zimbabwe, for example, one-third of the total land area was seized by white settlers. When Cecil Rhodes' Pioneer Column conquered the Ndebele kingdom in the west of the country in 1893, all of the

cattle in the country were taken as loot and the country was ruled by the British South Africa Company as the colony of Rhodesia. By tradition, all the cattle in the kingdom were nominally the property of the king. The British South Africa Company assumed that in defeating the king, they would inherit all of his property — including the cattle. It was hardly surprising that the Ndebele, primarily a cattle-keeping people, rose in rebellion against the confiscation of their livestock.

Rebellions by the Ndebele and the Shona peoples of Zimbabwe between 1896–1897 were finally suppressed by the white Rhodesian settlers. However, heroic memories of this first *Chimurenga* or freedom war lived on to inspire a second, this time successful, *Chimurenga* in the 1970s. Similarly, in West Africa the war of resistance against the French in northern Guinea and Ivory Coast lasted for 20 years and left a lasting impression on the peoples of the region.

The Nama and Herero peoples rose in rebellion between 1904 and 1905 against German occupation and seizure of their land and cattle in the German colony of South-West Africa (Namibia). For a while, the rebellion looked like it might succeed since German settlers were driven from their farms in the central highlands. Eventually, the arrival of a large, well-equipped army from Germany overcame both Nama

The Matabele War of 1893 is shown here as a heroic white defensive action. In fact it was a swift, well-armed invasion by Cecil Rhodes' British South Africa Company. The Ndebele (or Matabele) were forced to abandon their capital, Bulawayo, but struck back later in a major uprising in 1896.

The Herero Revolt in German South-West Africa (Namibia), 1904. Many such uprisings in this period were desperate African attempts to reverse the colonial conquest. Despite some early successes, they were all ultimately defeated by the European's superior weapons and their ability to ship in troops from abroad.

COMBAT SANGLANT DANS LE SUD-OUEST AFRICAIN
La garnison allemande de Windhoek, assiégée par les Herreros, débloquée

The Herero nation must leave the country. If it will not do so I shall compel it by force . . . . Inside German territory every Herero tribesman, armed or unarmed, with or without cattle, will be shot. No women and children will be allowed in the territory: they will be driven back to their people or fired on. These are the last words to the Herero nation from me, the great General of the mighty German Emperor.

Quoted in H. Bley, South West Africa under German Rule (London, 1971), pages 163-164

and Herero resistance. Thousands of Herero men, women, and children were driven into the eastern desert where many perished of thirst and starvation. A few made it to Ngamiland, in present-day Botswana, where the local people lent them land and cattle. There the Herero lived for several generations, keeping alive their traditions and dreams of freedom until their country won its independence in 1990. Since then large numbers of Botswana Herero have returned to their homeland of Namibia.

These and other stories of resistance kept alive traditions of a heroic past when Africans were independent of European overrule. All over the continent Africans never lost sight of their ability to rule themselves. Even in territories like the deserts of northern

Somalia, where Europeans were not interested in taking land for white settlement, the strength of Somali resistance between 1899 and 1920 was such that the British were unable to defeat the forces of Muhammed Abdille Hassan. The British called this formidable foe the "Mad Mullah" and used aerial bombardment to destroy Hassan's desert fortress of Taleh in 1920. Even then it was only the death of the Somali leader later that year that led to the collapse of direct Somali resistance.

REASONS FOR RESENTMENT

In the early years of colonial occupation, the European rulers were often very brutal in the way they exploited the peoples and resources of the continent. The most extreme example was Congo, then ruled by the Belgian king as the Congo Free State. Here the king's agents forced local villagers to collect bundles of dried rubber resin from the wild rubber trees of the forest. They were not paid for this and those that failed to provide the amount demanded had a hand cut off. The other colonial powers thought this practice excessive and in 1908 external pressure forced the Belgian king to hand over the territory to the Belgian government. The Belgians abolished this practice and other excesses of the king's regime, but the foundations for a deep resentment of European rule had already been laid and were still prevalent in 1960 when the Belgians withdrew from the Congo.

In the thirty-year period between 1890 and 1920 thousands of miles of railroad track were laid in tropical Africa. The main purpose of European colonial rule had been to gain access to the rich mineral and agricultural resources of this region. Thus in almost every case the railroad line was built from a seaport at

Alerted by British and American missionaries to the horrors of the Belgian King Leopold II's rule in the Congo, the British consul, Roger Casement, published a highly critical report in 1904. Here, Punch cartoonist Linley Sambourne provides his interpretation of Leopold's rule.

PUNCH, OR THE LONDON CHARIVARI.—November 28, 1906.

IN THE RUBBER COILS.

Scene.—*The Congo "Free" State.*

Each town in the district is forced to bring a certain quantity [of rubber] to the headquarters of the commissaire every Sunday. It is collected by force. The soldiers drive the people into the bush. If they will not go they are shot down, and their left hands cut off and taken as trophies to the commissaire. These hands, the hands of men, women and children, are placed in rows before the commissaire, who counts them to see that the soldiers have not wasted the cartridges.

Report by Rev. J. B. Murphy, American missionary, on the methods of rubber collection used in the Congo Free State, published in The Times, *London, November 18, 1895.*

the coast to a major inland source of raw material. In South Africa, Ghana, and Guinea the railroad lines led to gold mines. In Congo and Zambia, valuable copper was transported by rail, while in Senegal it was ground nuts, in northern Nigeria ground nuts and cotton, and in Uganda cotton.

THE *CORVÉE* SYSTEM

These modern methods of transportation were not introduced for the benefit of the Africans of the region as a whole, nor were they made at European expense. The railroad lines were built by forced labor. Local people living near the track were made to work, without being paid for their efforts. In French West Africa the forced-labor principle was extended to cover all government projects for most of the colonial period. Forced labor was known as the *corvée* system. Local chiefs were obliged to force all the men in their village to provide a certain amount of their labor free to the government every year. The system — a major source of African resentment — was not finally abolished until 1946.

TAXATION

The imposition of a poll tax, a requirement for voting, caused great resentment among Africans. The tax was adopted in almost every African country throughout the colonial period. It had to be paid in cash by each adult man. The amount was usually about $5 per annum or its equivalent. This may not seem very much to us today, but in those days it was considered a large sum of money. On the white-owned farms of central and East Africa it was the equivalent of one or two months' wages.

The purpose of the poll tax was twofold. It paid the cost of colonial administration by providing salaries for the European administrators and the police force. The tax also served to force Africans into the cash economy. For centuries the common trade currencies of the African interior were lengths of cloth, cowrie shells, glass beads, and copper ingots. Few Africans beyond the coastal ports had experience with European-style currencies before the colonial period.

In parts of East and West Africa, local peasants were able to earn currency by growing cash crops, such as ground nuts, cocoa, and cotton, for export to Europe. Others moved away from the rural areas to find low-paying jobs in the colonial administration. Many of them were taken on by the colonizers as housemen, clerical workers, or caretakers.

The majority of Africans, however, had always lived a self-sufficient existence, growing their own food, making their own tools, and building their own houses out of local materials. The cash economy was still important because of the need to pay taxes. Initially, many of them were compelled to seek work on the farms and mines of European settlers. Indirectly, therefore, the tax was a means of providing labor for European projects across the continent. Later on, these workers were able to find low-paying jobs in the developing urban areas.

The poll tax was felt by Africans to be one of the most unfair features of colonial rule, especially as it did not have to be paid by those European colonists who chose to settle in Africa. Africans felt that they were being forced to pay for their own colonization. Even in the most peaceful African countries this kept alive an underlying resentment of colonial overrule.

Many Africans were driven to seek waged employment in the European-owned mines. As shown in this photograph of 1888, Africans made up a large proportion of the workforce in the gold mine at De Kaap, eastern Transvaal, South Africa.

CHANGING TIMES

Africans learned an important lesson from the scramble for Africa. They realized that they had lost their freedom largely because of European technological superiority. They quickly recognized that the way to catch up on this technological deficiency was by means of European systems of education.

A MADAGASCAR
Leçons de culture aux indigènes

Here the French in Madagascar are shown instructing local farmers in cultivation methods. European colonists generally directed African farmers to cultivate new crops — usually those that would benefit Europe. Agricultural "experts" invariably ignored local indigenous farming knowledge, built upon centuries of experience, assuming — often wrongly — that their own "scientific" knowledge was superior.

By the 1920s, Europeans had begun to rationalize their rule over Africa. They claimed that they were in sole possession of the knowledge and expertise — the "superior civilization" — necessary to rule and

Le Petit Journal

ADMINISTRATION
61, RUE LAFAYETTE, 61

Les manuscrits ne sont pas rendus
On s'abonne sans frais
dans tous les bureaux de poste

5 CENT. SUPPLÉMENT ILLUSTRÉ 5 CENT.

22ᵐᵉ Année ———— Numéro 1.096

DIMANCHE 19 NOVEMBRE 1911

ABONNEMENTS

LA FRANCE VA POUVOIR PORTER LIBREMENT AU MAROC LA CIVILISATION
LA RICHESSE ET LA PAIX

This image of Morocco in 1911 illustrates the French view of why France was in Africa: as the source of civilization, prosperity and peace. For Africans, the reality was very different.

"modernize" the continent. In practice, of course, they wanted to remain in control of Africa because then they could rule it to their advantage, ensuring that the economies of Africa managed to answer to Europe's needs. Thus economic priorities were on the mining of minerals and the growing of plantation crops that would benefit the industries of Europe. Europeans were not in Africa to develop the continent for the benefit of Africans. It is clear that the new colonial governments were not interested in helping Africans become educated. If they did, then Europeans would lose the advantages that educational and technological superiority gave them. If Africans became their equals intellectually, might they not demand equal treatment economically, socially, and politically? In that case how long would Africans continue to accept European overrule?

EDUCATION AND THE ROLE OF THE MISSIONARIES

Unskilled African workers build a marketplace in German South West Africa. During the early years of colonization, Europeans discouraged education among Africans. They relied on the manpower of uneducated laborers to create the colonial infrastructure.

At first, colonial governments refused to fund African education. Christian missionaries, however, were prepared to fill the gap. European missionaries had been active in the coastal regions of Africa since the early nineteenth century. One of the most important centers of Christian mission activity was Freetown, the capital of Sierra Leone. Freetown had been founded in 1787 by 400 former African slaves who had gained their freedom in England. Having been forcibly divorced from their traditional African religious roots, they had become ardent Christians and were culturally very anglicized. Joined by European missionaries and other freed slaves in the early nineteenth century, the Freetown "Creoles" (Africans born abroad) built a strong Christian community. The community sent African missionaries all over coastal West Africa. Their most famous project was the Niger Mission, established in southern Nigeria in 1857 by the Church Missionary Society. The mission was led by the saintly African bishop, Samuel Ajayi Crowther, a pioneer of western education in the region.

74639

In the early years of colonization, Europeans greatly resented the presence of educated Africans. This was largely because they proved false the myth of European superiority. It is worth noting that when Bishop Crowther died in 1891 — by which time southern Nigeria had come under British rule— he was replaced as head of the Niger Mission by a European. There were at this time several educated African missionaries, qualified, ready, and able to take Bishop Crowther's place.

AFRICAN CHURCHES

In South Africa a number of educated Christians had broken away from the restrictive control of European missionaries and founded their own independent churches. This was known as the "Ethiopian Church" movement, taken from the Greek word "Ethiopia,"used to describe Africa in the Bible. Africans were often influenced and encouraged in this movement by American evangelists who came to South Africa in the late nineteenth century. They helped a number of Africans go to the United States for higher education at African-American teachers' colleges.

Following the spread of colonialism into central Africa, groups of African Christians similarly broke away from European controlled missions to found their own Christian churches. In the British colony of Nyasaland, present-day Malawi, Elliot Kamwana founded the Watchtower sect in 1908, as a missionary branch of the Jehovah's Witnesses. Kamwana preached the imminent "second coming" of Christ, who would liberate Africans from European oppression. Although Kamwana was arrested by the British authorities, the Watchtower movement spread to neighboring Southern Rhodesia, present-day Zimbabwe. Here it greatly disturbed the white settler community who had recently conquered the country.

Similarly, in 1921, Simon Kimbangu declared himself a prophet sent by God to deliver the people of the Belgian Congo from oppression. Kimbangu was promptly imprisoned by the Belgian authorities. However, "Kimbanguism" and a belief in imminent biblical deliverance from oppression lived on in the Congo throughout the 1920s and 1930s. Thereafter any crisis — such as a drought or the threat of famine — would provoke a brief revival.

Soon after the conquest of its West and Equatorial African empires, France was calling upon its new colonial subjects to fight and die for France in the trenches of the European western front during World War I in 1914-1918.

WORLD WAR I

World War I significantly affected many parts of Africa. In French West Africa, the French imposed forced military conscription. In all some 150,000 Africans were drafted into the French army, 30,000 of them died fighting in the trenches of the European western front. Opposition to conscription was fierce, and the French used military force to bring the region under more direct colonial control during this period of upheaval in Europe.

In East Africa the British and their Belgian allies invaded the German colony of Tanganyika and fought a long and destructive war throughout the 1914-1918 period. Both sides conscripted Africans as soldiers, porters, and laborers, and on the allied side alone an estimated 100,000 of these men died of injury, disease, or exhaustion.

British recruitment policies for the war in East Africa helped prompt a rebellion in Nyasaland in 1915. The rebels were led by the Reverend John Chilembwe — an American-educated African missionary. He had other specific grievances against local white settlers, but he added to his protest the shedding of innocent African blood in the war in East Africa. Declaring that he was prepared to "strike a blow and die" for African freedom, Chilembwe's rebellion expressed the frustration of someone who had tried to act for the betterment of his people and found himself still excluded from equal treatment and justice. The tiny rebellion was crushed, Chilembwe was killed, and his huge brick church building was destroyed. Nevertheless, memories of Chilembwe and his sacrifice lived on to inspire a new generation of Malawian nationalists in the 1950s.

When the war ended in 1918, an influenza epidemic swept across the continent, killing up to 3 percent of the African population. Europeans were widely blamed for the spread of the disease. There was some basis to this claim. The population was weakened by the devastation of war. The disease, previously unknown in most of Africa, spread along the new railroad lines. As a consequence of colonialism, the young men of isolated rural communities trekked for many miles in search of paid employment on white-owned plantations, farms, and mines (see page 17). Outbreaks of influenza often

Many natives are puzzling over the question how it can be possible that the whites, who brought them the Gospel of Love, are now murdering each other, and throwing to the winds the commands of the Lord Jesus . . . . How far the ethical and religious authority of the white man . . . is impaired by this war we shall only be able to measure later on. I fear that the damage done will be very considerable.

The medical missionary Albert Schweitzer, commenting on the psychological effects of World War I, from: On the Edge of the Primeval Forest (trans. C T Campion, London, 1922), page 138. Quoted in Melvin E Page (ed) Africa and the First World War, Macmillan, London, 1987, pages 18-19.

Although many African men were compelled to seek employment on the farms of white settlers, traditional, subsistence agriculture continued to be practiced all over the continent. In East Africa, shown here in 1904, women were always the farmers. Though their technology was simple, it was sufficient for their needs. The men were the soldiers, hunters, and cattle herders.

White farmers in Southern Rhodesia paid very low wages. To attract workers to their farms they allowed African families to settle and cultivate small plots for themselves. In return, at harvest time, as shown here, the whole family was expected to turn out and work, often unpaid, for the white settler.

occurred in their wake. It was also widespread in the crowded conditions of the mining compounds of Rhodesia, where an estimated 7 percent of the workers died.

BETWEEN THE WARS

In the interwar years of the 1920s and 1930s colonial administrators — finished now with conquest and establishing their right to rule — began to interfere more directly in the day-to-day life of African communities. They criticized African subsistence cultivation as backward and unproductive, but they made little money or expertise available to improve basic peasant farming. Instead, they pushed Africans into working on European settler plantations and in mines where wages were set deliberately low. Most of the mining companies discouraged family settlement in the new mining towns, preferring to use male migrant workers on short contracts. They could then pay a low "bachelor wage," on the assumption that the miner's family was being supported by subsistence agriculture at home.

As Africans reluctantly adapted to colonialism, gained some very basic education at mission schools, and learned more about the wider world, the hypocrisy of the colonial system became ever more apparent to them. In Kenya and Rhodesia, for instance, white settlers were given the best agricultural land. The government then offered them financial and technical assistance that was never made available to Africans. In Kenya, Africans were banned from growing crops that competed with those produced by European

It may interest you to know that to this day, unhulled coffee is known in Luganda as *kiboko*. The word *kiboko* means "whip." This name derives from the fact that prior to the 1930s, if a farmer disobeyed a colonial order to grow coffee, he would be whipped. This illustrates what I mean when I say that coffee became important to our economy as a result of colonial design and enforcement.

Yoweri Kaguta Museveni, President of Uganda, in an address to the International Coffee Organization, Kampala, November 20, 1989.

farmers. In Rhodesia, African cattle were not allowed to be sold directly at the country's European-controlled markets. The justification was that African cattle were not of sufficient quality and that they might carry disease. The only outlet for these cattle was to sell them to white farmers, at prices that were deliberately kept low. The hypocrisy of this arrangement became apparent when the animals were then freely marketed as white-owned cattle.

In the French zones, some Africans were allowed to become "assimilated" into French colonial society, provided they rejected their African cultural heritage and adopted French language and culture in its place. Most Africans were very reluctant to reject their own historic culture. Those who did try to achieve assimilation came up against enormous barriers. They were expected to achieve higher educational standards than the mass of European Frenchmen, and yet there were no institutions of higher education in French West or Equatorial Africa. In addition, Muslims found that Christian applicants were always given priority. This discrimination, which was a problem throughout the colonial period, resulted in a political conflict that has never really been resolved.

Of course, the French never intended that more than a tiny elite of Africans would become assimilated. They needed local African collaborators, through whom they could rule Africa; they did not need millions of African Frenchmen. The racist discrimination of colonialism in Africa had become very apparent by the 1930s, and it was one of the key reasons behind the early movement for independence.

In the 1920s at a French mission school in Cameroon. France took over most of Cameroon from Germany in 1919. The main emphasis of their lessons, like this one, was the French language. Note the wall map showing the vast expanse of French-ruled Africa.

WAR AND LIBERATION: 1935-1947

By the 1930s, despite the African desire for independence, European control of the continent seemed total. Yet, there had been earlier protests like the First Pan-African Congress in London, 1900, where Africans joined African-Americans and others from the Caribbean to protest against colonialism. However, the world was about to be totally transformed by World War II. Africa was to feel the war's effects strongly, and, for the first time, the influence of world politics was to tip the continental balance of power in Africa's favor.

ITALY INVADES ETHIOPIA

God and history will remember your judgement . . . . Are the States [of the League] going to set up the terrible precedent of bowing before force?

The Ethiopian Emperor Haile Selassie, addressing the General Assembly of the League of Nations in Geneva, his country, a founder member of the League, having just been conquered by Fascist Italy, May 1936. Quoted in K. Shillington, History of Africa (Revised ed, Macmillan, London, 1995).

World War II started in Europe in 1939. This was not so in Africa, where the battle against international Fascism began in 1935 with the Italian invasion of Ethiopia. The Italians had come late to the scramble for Africa. They had seized Libya from the failing Turkish Ottoman Empire in 1911, and they also held the northeastern coastal territories of Eritrea and southern Somalia. Their attempt to invade Ethiopia in 1896 had been halted by the modernized army of Emperor Menelik II. This made Ethiopia the only African country to successfully repel European military invasion during the scramble for Africa period. For the next 40 years most Africans probably remained unaware of this great Ethiopian achievement. They did not know that there remained at least one African country that had stood up to the European onslaught.

Between 1935 and 1936 news spread across Africa that Ethiopia was falling to the Italians. Although the Ethiopians managed to hold off the invasion for many months, the use of poisonous gas and aerial bombardment by the Italians finally defeated them.

Le Petit Journal

Le Petit Journal
Chaque jour 5 centimes
Le Supplément illustré
Chaque semaine 5 centimes

SUPPLÉMENT ILLUSTRÉ
Huit pages : CINQ centimes

ABONNEMENTS

Neuvième année   DIMANCHE 28 AOUT 1898   Numéro 406

Le Négus Ménélik à la bataille d'Adoua
TABLEAU DE M. Paul BUFFET (SALON DE 1898)

Menelik II, Emperor of Ethiopia, 1889-1913, built a strong, modernized army and actively expanded his empire during the European scramble for Africa. Here a French artist portrays him as a "Napoleon" of Africa, inflicting defeat on the Italians at the battle of Adowa in March 1896.

Haile Selassie, the Emperor of Ethiopia, was forced into exile. He went to the League of Nations headquarters in Geneva to seek support. As a founding member of the League, Selassie clearly expected his fellow member states to uphold Ethiopia's right to independence. He was disappointed. Great Britain and France, the League's major powers, did no more than impose a limited arms and fuel embargo on Italy. This policy had no effective result in Ethiopia.

The conquest of Ethiopia had a profound impact on the African psyche and aroused great indignation across the continent. When World War II broke out in 1939, Britain and its Allies had little problem recruiting Africans for an Allied force to liberate Ethiopia. In 1941 Haile Selassie returned to southern Sudan to

November 1935, one month into the Italian invasion of Ethiopia, Eritreans in northern Ethiopia (near Adowa) are obliged to salute a portrait of the Italian Fascist dictator Benito Mussolini. At the time the invasion was being held up by stiff Ethiopian resistance.

head a force of Ethiopian patriots. Meanwhile, the British recruited thousands of African troops from Nigeria, Ghana, and Sierra Leone, and a mixture of African and white-settler forces moved up to Kenya from Rhodesia and Nyasaland. Within five months the Ethiopian capital, Addis Ababa, had been retaken, and Haile Selassie was restored to his throne. Desperate for continued African support in the war against Germany, Britain agreed to withdraw its occupying forces from Ethiopia and recognize Ethiopian independence.

THE ATLANTIC CHARTER

The liberation of Ethiopia was a symbol of hope for the continent and had an enormous effect on African attitudes to World War II and its purpose. From an African viewpoint, the purpose of the war was the restoration of freedom to occupied territories. Their interpretation of what constituted an occupied territory, however, was very different from that of the European colonial powers. Africans were greatly encouraged in their belief by the publication of the Atlantic Charter. This was a declaration of principles signed by British Prime Minister Winston Churchill and President Franklin D.

Roosevelt in 1941, just before the United States entered the war. In it the two leaders referred to the sovereign rights of nations and to the point that self-government should be restored to all those who had been forcibly deprived of it. Africans interpreted this as referring to the colonial occupation of Africa. The United States also intended that the principles should ultimately be applied to Africa. To some extent this was because European colonial empires deprived American agriculture and industry of access to huge potential markets and resources. When African journalists published their interpretation of the Atlantic Charter, however, Churchill made it clear that Britain intended it to refer only to European territories occupied by Italy or Germany, and not to Africa. Nevertheless, the African appetite had been whetted, and the United States was seen in Africa as a potential ally.

The Atlantic Charter, signed by President Franklin D. Roosevelt and the British Prime Minister Winston Churchill (seen here aboard a British warship off Newfoundland) in August 1941, agreed in principle to the right of all peoples to choose their own government. Africans saw the Charter as signaling an end to colonialism.

AFRICANS AT WAR

African troops served in the Allied forces in North Africa and Italy between 1942 and 1943. They also fought in the Far Eastern campaign, where they served with distinction fighting for the British against the Japanese in the forests of Burma. Throughout these campaigns, Africans found themselves fighting alongside whites in a universal struggle for "freedom and democracy." With this experience, they could not return to their colonial African territories after the war and

Italian wartime propaganda showing the alleged effect of an Italian attack on a Kenyan border fort. The British officers flee, leaving their African troops to do the fighting. Published on August 4, 1940, two months after British defeat in northern France and five months before British — and African — troops began the liberation of Ethiopia.

4 agosto 1940
A. XVIII - N 22

LA TRIBUNA ILLUSTRATA

Metodi di guerra inglesi. — Nel Kenia, mentre le nostre truppe sferravano un violento, irresistibile attacco contro il forte Harrington che difendeva il paese di Mojale, gli ufficiali inglesi fuggivano da quella posizione sulle loro automobili, lasciando a proteggere il forte soltanto le truppe di colore. Poco dopo la nostra bandiera sventolava su quell'importante punto strategico. (Disegno di VITTORIO PISANI)

meekly submit to the indignities of poverty-level wages and colonial discrimination.

As many as 80,000 Africans from the French empire served in France from the outbreak of war to the fall of France to German invasion in 1940. Thereafter, some French colonial governors in Africa submitted to the Vichy regime, while others, led by the black governor of Chad, Félix Eboué from French Guiana in South America, declared support for the exiled "Free French" government of Charles de Gaulle. Briefly, in 1943, the French Congo capital of Brazzaville was in effect the capital of "Free France" itself. In January 1944, before the Allied invasion of France later that year, De Gaulle held a Free French conference at Brazzaville, but, significantly, he did not invite any Africans to the conference, and the future of France's African empire was not — yet — up for discussion.

THE NEED FOR CHANGE

When peace finally came in 1945, Britain and France — the old imperial powers — were economically and psychologically exhausted. They needed to focus all their efforts on economic recovery, and this made them more dependent than ever on the resources of their African empires. During the war colonial administrators had persuaded or pressured Africans into producing more copper, tin, ground nuts, palm oil, rubber, sisal, and cotton. These were all vital raw materials for the Allied war effort. The colonial powers were obliged to recognize that Africa had made a considerable contribution to the war, both in terms of materials and of troops. They realized that from now on they would have to seek greater cooperation and consent if European rule was to continue in Africa.

How long would Africans be willing to accept European overrule? After the war France and Britain found themselves displaced as the world's superpowers. They could no longer afford to hold reluctant empires against their will. Potential African leaders were now much more aware of world events. They observed that the peoples of India had been granted a degree of self-government in 1939. African hopes were raised by the speed with which this was to lead to complete sovereign independence for India and Pakistan in 1947. As Africa's political leaders saw it, if Britain would part with India, the greatest jewel in her imperial crown, then independence for Africa could not be far behind.

Barrels of palm oil awaiting shipment from a port in the Niger Delta in the 1920s. Nigerian palm oil continued to be the basic raw material for margarine and soap in wartime Britain.

AFRICAN NATIONALISM

A Belgian Protestant missionary baptizes converts in the Congo in 1904. Although usually independent of colonial governments, Christian missions played an important role in undermining indigenous African culture and beliefs, thus helping to promote African acceptance of colonial rule.

The period before World War II in Africa had seen the gradual emergence of a class of educated Africans. They attended mission schools and used their new knowledge to get jobs in the colonial administration as clerks and interpreters, or to become teachers themselves.

By this time education had become more widely available in colonial Africa. During the 1920s and 1930s a number of elementary schools had been set up and funded entirely by Africans. The French provided a certain amount of elementary education in their African colonies, but it was focused almost exclusively on teaching the French language. Those who sought higher education were expected to go to France for it and become culturally "assimilated." The Belgians and Portuguese left education entirely in the hands of

missionaries whose teaching was limited to basic literacy and mathematical skills. The Belgians positively discouraged anything beyond the most rudimentary primary education for Africans.

In the Gold Coast (now Ghana) the British set up Achimota College, outside Accra. This was the first government-funded secondary school in Africa. It was primarily intended to produce pupils suited to becoming African clerks and lower-ranking officers in the ever-expanding colonial civil service. Through links with London University, Achimota also offered a degree course in engineering. Fourah Bay College, the former mission college in Freetown, Sierra Leone, also offered degree courses in certain subjects. It was linked to Durham University in Britain.

AN EDUCATED ELITE

In this way, some Africans began to gain limited access to higher education. Many of them had to go abroad to find suitable colleges. At Fourah Bay College during the 1930s, for example, half of the students were Nigerian. The cost of attending a college of higher education was prohibitive for all but a very small privileged elite. Nevertheless, by the outbreak of World War II in 1939, many countries had a small group of professionally-qualified Africans. This was particularly noticeable in West and South Africa, where many Africans became doctors, lawyers, teachers, and newspaper editors.

In Sierra Leone, Gold Coast, and Nigeria this elite of western-educated men could be traced back through several generations. It originated in the days of the pioneer African missionaries in the mid-nineteenth century. In South Africa a class of educated Africans emerged even earlier. By the end of the nineteenth century there were already several newspapers in South Africa produced by Africans. It is hardly surprising, therefore, that the first African nationalist political party was founded in South Africa in 1912. Originally called the South African Native National Congress, it changed its name to the African National Congress (ANC) in 1923.

The ANC was not a revolutionary group. It was made up of lawyers, doctors, journalists, teachers, and chiefs — a potential African middle class. Their primary goal was to end racial discrimination in South

Africa through peaceful means. Most of the educated elite all over Africa merely wanted to be treated as equals at this stage. They wanted to take part in running their own affairs, alongside the colonials. But wherever they turned, they were frustrated.

It was largely in French West Africa — and especially in the coastal towns of Senegal — that Africans could take up positions of responsibility within the colonial structure. Here the French policy of limited "assimilation" worked most effectively. A small number of educated Africans were eventually accepted by French colonial society and were able to climb the promotion ladder of the French colonial civil service.

STRIVING AGAINST INJUSTICE

The overwhelming tone of the interwar years was one of Africans learning how to come to terms with the colonial situation. Gone were the attempts to stop or

In Ghana, clerks and lower-ranking officers in the colonial civil service were trained at Achimota College. Like the French in West Africa, the British practiced a policy of limited assimilation in Ghana. This marine policeman was photographed in 1925, directing traffic at the end of the coast road in Accra.

Miners employed in the Northern Rhodesian copper mines suffered low pay, insanitary housing, poor diet, increased taxes, and racial discrimination. African nationalism drew on a deep well of grievance in the copperbelt during the postwar years.

reverse it. Now Africans were working within the system and earning a living to support their families. Nevertheless, they did not passively accept the harsh injustices of colonialism. Those with any degree of education were constantly striving to rid the system of injustice. Thus, although all forms of trade union activity were illegal, workers periodically staged spontaneous demonstrations to demand better pay and working conditions. Strikes took place in the mines and on the railroads of Guinea, Gold Coast, and Sierra Leone during the 1920s and 1930s and in the copper mines of Northern Rhodesia (Zambia) in 1935 and 1940. The cocoa farmers of Gold Coast, small-scale African producers, formed a federation and withheld their cocoa harvests in the 1930s until coastal merchants increased their prices.

All over tropical Africa self-help welfare associations were formed between the wars. The groups were often made up of migrant workers who originally came from the same rural district. There was no government social security in colonial Africa, and these groups helped their members in times of trouble.

In due course, people began to realize that small-scale local action was not enough. Real and lasting social justice could only be achieved through changes on a national level. The government in Africa had to change in order to represent the interests of Africans rather than those of imperial Europe. It was the educated elite, of African doctors, lawyers, teachers, and journalists, with their sophistication and experience to transform their local activity into agitation at a national level. Kenya's Jomo Kenyatta, secretary of a Kikuyu welfare association, took on an important national role at this time.

In the early years, before World War II, these leaders were not seeking political independence from Britain, France, Belgium, or Portugal. At first, they sought little more than social justice and some level of power-sharing with colonial authorities. The British and French were ready to place a few Africans on governing bodies, but they only appointed "moderates" they believed would not insist on too many changes. In 1914 the French did place one African representative on the French legislature in Paris. Portuguese and Belgian authorities were not prepared to make even these minor concessions. Even the British and French were very reluctant to agree to any form of popular elections. By allowing elections they would be authorizing a shift in the balance of power away from the colonials and toward the African people. Nevertheless, both governments thought that they could afford to make a few concessions. They believed that they could allow some level of self-government without losing control of their African colonies. Once political concessions began, however, the logic of independence could no longer be resisted. Even Belgium and Portugal, the least flexible of the colonial powers, were not immune to the pressures of African nationalist sentiment, which swept across the continent in the 1950s and 1960s.

After independence, old colonials often spoke as though the whole purpose of colonization in Africa had been to prepare Africans for self-government in the modern world. In reality, the lack of preparation for African independence was one of the greatest failings of the whole colonial enterprise. African independence did not come about as a result of colonial planning and foresight. Independence was won rather than granted. The imperial powers were weakening, and Africans seized the initiative.

It may take generations, or even centuries, for the peoples in some parts of the colonial empire to achieve self-government. But it is a major part of our policy, even among the most backward peoples of Africa, to teach them always to be able to stand a little more on their own feet.

Malcolm MacDonald, British Colonial Secretary, Hansard, *December 7, 1938.*

THE BIRTH OF INDEPENDENCE

EGYPT LEADS THE WAY

The African independence movement saw its first victory in Egypt in the years immediately following World War II. Egyptian civilians had suffered a great deal at the hands of the British who had requisitioned cotton, corn, camels, and workers during the war. The level of discontent in Egypt was high. When the British rejected peaceful demands for political independence, they were faced with strikes and riots by the Egyptians in Alexandria and Cairo. As a result, the British agreed to a limited form of independence in 1922. Sultan Fuad was declared king, but the British army remained in occupation and in control behind the scenes.

Sultan Fuad, seen here in his Cairo palace in 1914, was descended from the Mamluk Turks who had ruled Egypt for centuries. He was declared king in 1922. He and his son and successor Farouk (who ruled between 1936 and 1952) presided over one of the most corrupt regimes in twentieth-century Africa.

INDEPENDENCE IN NORTH AFRICA

Following World War II, Britain and France began to scale down their wartime military occupation of North Africa. Libya, under British military occupation since 1943, gained its independence in 1951. In 1952, the British handed over the coastal Muslim state of Eritrea to Ethiopia. By doing this they hoped to build a strong alliance with Christian Ethiopia in the face of rising Muslim power in the region. However, the British also succeeded in laying the foundations for one of Africa's longest civil wars, only to be resolved by Eritrean independence in 1993. Tunisia and Morocco got their independence from France in 1956, and the British withdrew from Sudan in the same year.

The British finally ended their military occupation of Egypt after World War II. This enabled a group of

The revolution that overthrew the corrupt and autocratic regime of Egypt's King Farouk began in February 1952 with riots and attacks, such as this on the British Embassy in Cairo. Britain was seen as the power behind the throne in Egypt.

Egyptian army officers to stage a coup against the corrupt regime of King Farouk in 1952. Two years later, Colonel Abdul Nasser took over as President of Egypt, and in 1956 he nationalized the Suez canal which had hitherto belonged to a French company. Nasser hoped to use the profits from the canal to build a new dam at Aswan. The dam was to provide the electricity needed both for industry and for irrigation by the farmers of the Nile valley. The British and French intervened, sending in troops to try and stop the nationalization. They faced tough opposition, however, from the Egyptian army, and they failed to get the backing of the United States, which wanted to see an end to European colonial rule in Africa.

SUEZ MARKS THE END OF THE COLONIAL ERA

The defeat of the British and French at Suez in 1956 sent out an important signal to the rest of the continent — European rule in Africa was coming to an end. France and Britain, too, largely accepted the lessons of Suez. From now on it was just a matter of negotiating how and when independence should take place. From the British and French points of view, however, the exception lay in those countries with substantial numbers of European settlers. Africans believed that there should be no exceptions. If anything, the countries with European settlers had even greater need of independence, for that was where Africans had suffered the worst levels of exploitation and discrimination. If European settlers refused to accept this, then they would have to be fought.

The main French settler colony was Algeria. In 1945 there were as many as 2 million French colonists in Algeria. They were determined that Algeria would not follow the path to independence of neighboring Tunisia and Morocco. The majority Muslim population, however, had been humiliated and treated as second-class citizens for the better part of a hundred years. They were determined to take power and to achieve complete independence. Following the violent suppression of peaceful Muslim demonstrations, Algerian nationalists launched an all-out war of liberation in 1954. By 1958 there were half a million French troops in Algeria, fighting a war which, by then, they clearly

With the withdrawal of the [British and French] invaders, Nasser's triumph was complete. No African leader in modern times has ever enjoyed so spectacular a diplomatic victory over European intruders. There could be no hesitation now about taking over the fifteen thousand British and French firms and other establishments to be found in Egypt, together with the massive British base in the canal zone. By January, 1957, Egypt was free at last of the excessive influence of Western European powers.

R Hallett, Africa Since 1875, *(Heinemann, London, 1975).*

could not win. The war in Algeria was to have a profound effect upon French colonial policy in the rest of Africa, as we shall see in the following chapter.

KENYA AND THE "MAU MAU"

The main British settler colonies were Kenya and Rhodesia, and the Rhodesian experience will be considered in the following chapter. In Kenya, white settlement was confined largely to the fertile highlands near the capital, Nairobi. Here African farmers, mainly Kikuyu, had been ousted from their ancestral lands earlier in the century to make way for huge white-settler estates.

The Kikuyu were pushed into infertile resettlement areas or overcrowded "reserves." It was among these people that a secret society grew up, sworn to secrecy in a series of oaths known as "Mau Mau." They hoped to persuade white settlers to abandon their farms by setting fire to crops and farm buildings and maiming farm animals. Gradually the scale of violence increased, and when a white farming family was killed in 1952, the colonial government declared a state of emergency. Hundreds of African nationalists were arrested — including Jomo Kenyatta. But "Mau Mau" was not part of the regular African nationalist movement, and the struggle escalated into full-scale war. Calling themselves the "African Land and Freedom Army," the Mau Mau fighters took to the forests, and the British brought in hundreds of troops from abroad. The forest fighters were eventually overcome, and the state of emergency was lifted in 1959. By then the British had realized that they must start negotiating with African nationalists for majority rule.

GOLD COAST INDEPENDENCE

In 1947 a number of African businessmen and lawyers in the Gold Coast formed the United Gold Coast Convention (UGCC). Kwame Nkrumah, a former teacher, was elected Secretary General — one of the most powerful positions in the new party. The UGCC demanded that the colony's constitution be revised to allow an elected African majority in the Legislative Council. When the colonial police opened fire on a peaceful demonstration of African ex-servicemen in 1948, there

When the "Mau Mau" rebellion broke out in Kenya in 1952, the British wrongly believed that it was organized by African nationalist politicians. Here, nationalist leader Jomo Kenyatta is seen under arrest. After many years in jail, Kenyatta was released and became the first president of independent Kenya.

was rioting in the streets of the colony's major towns. The UGCC was banned, and its leading members were imprisoned.

On his release after eight weeks in prison, Nkrumah founded a new, more radical, Convention People's Party (CPP). The party pursued complete independence by promoting a series of strikes and demonstrations across the country. Nkrumah was rearrested, but this time the British agreed to revise the constitution as the UGCC had originally demanded. In elections held in 1951, the CPP won a clear majority. Nkrumah was released from prison to become the leader of government business in the new parliament. At this point half the seats in parliament were still filled by colonial nominees, but by 1954 a new constitution had been drawn up, bringing fully-elected, internal self-government to the Gold Coast. CPP won the election, Nkrumah became prime minister and the Gold Coast became independent as the new state of Ghana in March 1957.

Nkrumah and his party had the mass of the people behind them . . . . Without Nkrumah, the Constitution [of 1951] would be still-born, and . . . there would no longer be any faith in the good intentions of the British Government. . . . the Gold Coast would be plunged into disorders, violence and bloodshed.

Governor Arden-Clarke, justifying his release of Nkrumah after the latter's election victory of 1951, African Affairs, London, January 1958.

"WIND OF CHANGE": 1958-1968

FRENCH COLONIAL REFORM

The French were always determined to dictate the pace of change in tropical Africa. This would allow them to retain a large measure of influence on the continent no matter what political changes occurred. The small elite of culturally assimilated Africans accepted in principle the idea of continued French imperial links, but sought a greater level of internal self-government in Africa. (See page 25 for French assimilation policy.) French colonial reforms of 1946 allowed tropical Africa to send ten elected delegates to the National Assembly in Paris. Among those elected were Léopold Senghor of Senegal and Félix Houphouët-Boigny of Ivory Coast. Both became leaders of their respective countries on the achievement of independence.

The French government was put under pressure by the war in Algeria. (See page 39.) As a result, further reforms were introduced, bringing fully-elected internal self-government to West and Equatorial Africa in 1956. France, however, retained control of African military and foreign affairs and economic development planning. The newly-elected African governments pressed for greater independence.

In ever greater trouble in Algeria, General de Gaulle, who came to power in France in 1958, decided to anticipate any future problems in tropical Africa by offering a referendum: "Yes," for continuing links with France and a promise of greater independence at some unspecified date in the future or "No," for immediate independence and a severing of all links with France. Faced with such a stark choice, all but Guinea voted "Yes." Thus Guinea became independent in 1958 and de Gaulle withdrew all French personnel and

equipment overnight, virtually bankrupting the newly independent state.

The other 14 French tropical African colonies got their independence, but with continuing French economic and diplomatic links, in 1960. The economic relationship between France and her former colonies was linked to the Communauté Financière Africaine, (CFA), or to the French franc, which had been the common currency across French Africa. The CFA could be exchanged at a guaranteed rate against the French franc. This arrangement has remained in place since independence, tying African import and export economies closely to France. At the same time, it has also provided the secure financial environment necessary for regular French investment in Africa.

In Algeria the war dragged on until the French were finally forced into a negotiated peace. They withdrew their armed forces, and Algeria became independent in 1962. Many of the French colonists returned to France bitter and disillusioned.

Muslims in Algeria had been granted limited local government voting rights in 1947. However, the country was still dominated by French colonial settlers who were backed by the army. Here a French settler, known as a colon, *supervises Muslim voters in 1958.*

BELGIAN WITHDRAWAL FROM AFRICA

The Belgians in the Congo had not even contemplated African self-government until 1956, when they decided to allow limited local elections in some of the

President Mobutu Sese Seko in Kinshasa, 1967. Mobutu was promoted by the Belgians from sergeant to colonel and made Army Chief of Staff just before the Congo's independence in 1960. Supported by Belgium and the United States, he seized power in 1965 and changed the country's name to Zaire in 1971.

major towns. The elections finally took place in 1958. After many years of government by an oppressive colonial regime, the local elections opened a floodgate of political activity, and an enormous number of regionally-based political parties were formed. The aspiring politicians were totally unrealistic, both in their demands for immediate independence and in the false promises that they made to the electorate. Political rallies during 1959 degenerated into riots and attacks on European property. The Belgians panicked, fearing another Algeria, and summoned the leaders of the main political parties to Belgium in January 1960. The African politicians were amazed when, with no further argument, the Belgians offered complete independence within five months. There had been no preparation for independence. As a result, when it came in June 1960, the army mutinied, and the country quickly disintegrated into lawlessness and civil war.

THE SHARPEVILLE MASSACRE

At the beginning of 1960, British Prime Minister Harold Macmillan made a tour through Africa. Throughout his tour, which began in newly-independent Ghana and ended in South Africa, Macmillan was particularly impressed by the strength and passion of African nationalist sentiments. In a speech to the all-white South African parliament, Macmillan referred to "the wind of change." This was the phrase that he used to describe the independence movement that was sweeping across Africa. He believed that the whole continent would eventually be affected, even South Africa. His white South African hosts were none too pleased by his implied criticism of their racially segregated and discriminatory society. On March 21, 1960, only a few weeks after Macmillan made his speech, police opened fire on an unarmed demonstration in a township named Sharpeville. They killed 69 men and women and wounded another 180. Most of the victims were shot in the back as they fled. It was following this massacre that the South African government banned the African National Congress (ANC) and all other African political parties. This forced African politicians such as Nelson Mandela, Walter Sisulu, and Oliver Tambo, to go underground and reluctantly resort to a campaign of violent sabotage.

The most striking of all the impressions I have formed since I left London a month ago is of the strength of . . . African national consciousness. In different places it may take different forms. But it is happening everywhere. The wind of change is blowing through this Continent.

British Prime Minister, Harold Macmillan, in a speech to the South African parliament, February 1960.

INDEPENDENCE IN THE BRITISH COLONIES

Broadly speaking, the achievement of independence in British West and East African colonies followed the Ghanaian pattern. By 1960, the British government had decided that the forces of African nationalism were too powerful to resist. Britain understood that their continued diplomatic and economic advantage in Africa depended upon a smooth transition to independence.

Nigeria, the largest and most populous state in tropical Africa, became independent in 1960. It was followed by Tanzania and Sierra Leone in 1961, Uganda in 1962, and finally Kenya in 1963. By 1968 the smaller British colonies of The Gambia, Botswana, Lesotho, Swaziland, and Mauritius had all achieved their independence.

UDI IN RHODESIA

... of all the Europeans of Central Africa, those of Southern Rhodesia have the worst antipathy towards Africans .... They look upon the Africans as inferior beings, with no right to a dignified and refined existence and fit only as hewers of wood and drawers of water for Europeans .... Under the Government provided by Southern Rhodesia, the relationship between us and the authorities will be one of slaves and masters, and the cardinal principle ... domination.

Dr. Hastings Kamusu Banda and Harry Nkumbula, to the British government, protesting about the proposed federation of the Rhodesias and Nyasaland, May 1, 1949. Quoted in R. I. Rotberg, The Rise of Nationalism in Central Africa, Harvard, 1964, page 224.

In Southern Rhodesia the white settler population tried to stand up to change by forming a federation with Northern Rhodesia and Nyasaland in 1953. They thought that profits from the copper mines of Northern Rhodesia and cheap labor from Nyasaland could be combined to subsidize and sustain the white settlers. African nationalist protests, boycotts, and mass actions were so effective in the northern colonies, however, that the federation broke up in 1963. Northern Rhodesia and Nyasaland then became independent in 1964, taking the names of Zambia and Malawi respectively.

Still determined to defy the trend, the Southern Rhodesian colonists, under the leadership of Ian Smith, made a Unilateral Declaration of Independence (UDI) in November 1965. They banned African nationalist political parties, locked up their leaders and began to implement the kind of racist discriminatory legislation that was already a feature in neighboring South Africa. In the absence of any effective assistance from the British government, African nationalists in Rhodesia reluctantly concluded that they would have to fight a guerrilla war if they were ever to liberate their country from the injustice and oppression of rule by local white colonists.

Rebel Rhodesian prime minister Ian Smith reads international reaction to his illegal UDI, November 1965. Smith tried to maintain the fiction that he was still loyal to the British Queen. He claimed that her government's policy of African majority rule was a betrayal of British citizens in the colonies.

A CONTINENT TRANSFORMED

By 1970, the political map of Africa showed a continent quite transformed. Gone forever were the great splashes of British imperial pink and the green or purple of France's African empire. The parts of Africa remaining under colonial rule were mainly concentrated in the south, although Portugal, Africa's oldest European imperial power, still held the tiny West African states of Guinea-Bissau and the Cape Verde Islands, off the coast of Senegal.

By 1970 most of the continent had already achieved independence from the colonial powers of Europe. Within five years Portugal had also withdrawn from Africa.

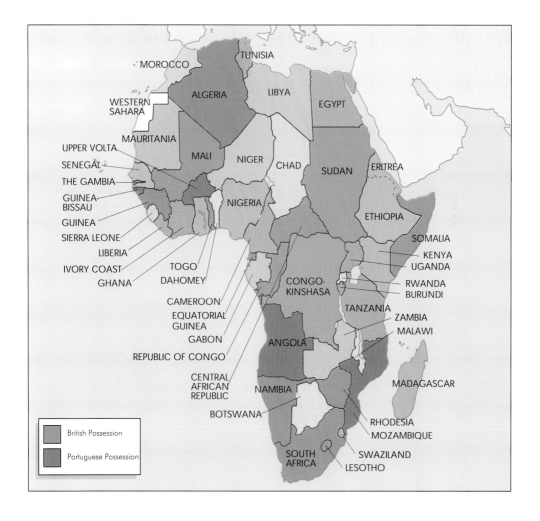

British Possession

Portuguese Possession

General Antonio de Spinola, future President of Portugal, on patrol in Guinea-Bissau, 1970. Portuguese propaganda issued with this photograph claimed the government had the "support of the natives." In fact, by September 1973, the guerrilla forces of Amilcar Cabral controlled so much of mainland Guinea that they proclaimed its independence.

By 1970, all of the remaining colonial governments in the south of the continent were facing various degrees of threat from determined guerrilla forces.

It was no coincidence that the continent's remaining colonial territories were all neighbors of South Africa — for it was South Africa that gave them political, economic, and military support. South Africa was the continent's most industrialized and economically powerful state. Here, 4 million whites owned 86 percent of the land and ruled more than 20 million blacks through the notoriously oppressive system of apartheid or "separateness."

AN END TO PORTUGUESE IMPERIALISM

Portugal's main interests were in their huge southern colonies of Mozambique and Angola. The Portuguese, always the weakest of the colonial powers, had themselves been ruled by a Fascist dictatorship since 1928. Their African colonies had always been regarded as an important prop to the weak, mostly rural economy of Portugal. It was the Portuguese, therefore, who were most threatened by the African liberation armies. Portuguese oppression had driven African nationalist forces underground in the early 1960s. By the 1970s it was becoming clear to the Portuguese military officers on the spot that the war was bleeding Portugal dry. General Spinola, who served as Portuguese commander in Guinea-Bissau from 1968 to 1973, recognized that the war against the nationalist forces could not be won. He believed that the sooner the Portuguese withdrew from Africa the better it would be for their home country. Spinola became the leader of a group of army officers who overthrew the Portuguese government by military coup in April 1974. In this instance, the African liberation struggle had helped to topple a European Fascist dictatorship.

After Spinola's coup, the Portuguese withdrew from Africa fairly quickly. Guinea-Bissau gained independence in September 1974, and Angola and Mozambique followed in 1975. In Mozambique the Portuguese handed over power to the victorious FRELIMO forces. Under the leadership of Samora Machel, FRELIMO had already occupied a large part of the country. In Angola there were several rival armies vying for power on the withdrawal of the Portuguese. The strongest was the Russian-backed MPLA, but they were opposed from the south by UNITA, which had the backing of South Africa and, indirectly, the United States. At the end of 1975, the South Africans invaded Angola, hoping to drive out the Socialist MPLA and install a UNITA government that would be an ally rather than an enemy of South Africa. The MPLA called for the support of a large, well-armed Cuban army that forced a South African withdrawal, but the foundations had been laid for a bitter civil war that was to devastate Angola for the next 20 years.

In July 1975, as the Portuguese begin their withdrawal from Angola, the Russian-backed MPLA are firmly in control of the capital, Luanda. In southern Angola, the anti-communist forces of UNITA (seen here) appeal through Western journalists (right of picture) for U.S. weapons and logistical support.

Much as we in Botswana would have preferred peaceful change in Rhodesia (for which we have worked so hard) to violent revolution, we have now accepted that it would be unrealistic for us to expect peaceful change in a situation where the oppressors of our people prefer war to peace.

Sir Seretse Khama, President of Botswana, speaking at Oxford University, June 4, 1976, quoted in Seretse Khama, 1921-1980, by Parsons, Henderson and Tlou (Macmillan, Gaborone, 1995), page 329.

THE FRONT LINE STATES

The collapse of the Portuguese empire marked a turning point in the history of southern Africa and the fight for liberation. The region most immediately affected was the rebel colony of Rhodesia, which was now almost completely surrounded by the independent, African-ruled countries of Botswana, Zambia, and Mozambique. The leaders of these three countries were now joined by those of Angola and Tanzania to form an informal grouping called the Front Line States. Their aim was to assist and coordinate support for the liberation forces of Zimbabwe (the African name for Rhodesia), Namibia, and South Africa. The main focus was initially on Zimbabwe where they believed, with good reason, there was the greatest chance of success.

The liberation forces of Zimbabwe had been operating from exile in Zambia and Tanzania for many years. Now that Mozambique was independent, they were able to use its long border to infiltrate the country. Their military successes mounted, and by late 1979 they controlled most of the country outside the main cities. The Smith regime was forced to recognize defeat. At this point the British government, which had done little to put a stop to the UDI rebellion since 1965 (see page 46), reassumed control of the rebel colony. A constitutional conference was held in London that led to full and free elections in February 1980 and independence for Zimbabwe two months later. The former guerrilla leader Robert Mugabe became prime minister.

NAMIBIA

The spotlight now turned on South Africa and Namibia. The vast desert expanse of Namibia in the southwest had been occupied by South Africa since it defeated the German colonists there in 1915. Since World War II, South African occupation of Namibia was in defiance of a United Nations mandate.

The Namibian liberation force, the SWAPO, had been fighting South African occupation of their country since 1960. Since 1976 they had been operating from Angola, but Angola was in the throes of a civil war. The SWAPO suffered periodic South African raids and constant attacks from South Africa's ally, UNITA (see page 49). In early 1988, however, a South African

Celebrating Namibia's independence from South Africa in Windhoek, 1990. The date for Independence Day, March 21, was chosen in memory of those South Africans who had died at the Sharpeville massacre 30 years before.

force was surrounded and facing defeat in southern Angola. At the same time, the South African government faced a simmering rebellion in the urban areas of South Africa itself. At last, they were forced to the negotiating table. In return for a phased Cuban withdrawal from Angola, the South Africans agreed to end their illegal occupation of Namibia. This led fairly quickly to free elections in Namibia in 1989, which were won by SWAPO. Namibian independence came in March 1990.

SOUTH AFRICA

South Africa itself presented a unique situation. Here there was no foreign power that could be persuaded to withdraw and acknowledge African independence. South Africa had been occupied by white settlers for several centuries. During the nineteenth century, when it was largely a colony of Britain, the remaining independent African kingdoms of the region had been defeated and the best part of their lands taken for further white settlement. In 1910, the British government granted virtual independence to South Africa, leaving the white minority of settlers to rule the country as they wished. Successive white governments imposed increasingly oppressive legislation that was aimed primarily at keeping the land, wealth, and government of the country firmly in white hands. The South African security forces were so powerful and so firmly in control that it was very difficult for the exiled African liberation forces to mount an effective campaign of

The state of the 15 million children under the age of five who live in countries bordering on the Republic of South Africa is grave, and getting worse. They are caught up in externally supported civil conflict and economic destabilization which they are too young to understand or counter.

From Children on the Frontline, *UNICEF Report, 1989, quoted in* Apartheid Terrorism, the Destabilization Report *(The Commonwealth Secretariat, London, 1989),* page 11.

sabotage and guerrilla warfare. Nevertheless, within the country, African civilians, who numbered an estimated 35 million by the late 1980s, conducted more and more effective campaigns of civil disobedience and defiant demonstrations through much of the 1980s.

In 1989, following their defeat in Angola and withdrawal from Namibia, the South African government was finally forced to recognize the inevitable: It would have to negotiate the future of South Africa with the leaders of the African majority. In February 1990 the ban was lifted on the ANC and other African political parties, and African political prisoners were released, among them Nelson Mandela who had been imprisoned for 27 years. There followed four years of intensive constitutional negotiations leading to South Africa's first free, non-racial elections and the inauguration of Mandela as President in May 1994.

August 1988. Defeated South African forces withdraw from southern Angola, across the Kunene River to Namibia. South African defeat in Angola and subsequent withdrawal from Namibia was a crucial step along the road to the liberation of South Africa itself.

THE POLITICAL LEGACY

The African politicians who inherited the responsibilities of government at independence faced enormous political problems. The 54 countries into which the continent is divided were almost all totally artificial creations — products of the scramble for Africa in the late nineteenth century. (See page 9.) A large number of political boundaries appear as straight lines on the map (see page 11), especially those across the more remote regions of the Sahara. Those that are not straight lines tend to follow the line of rivers or the watersheds between river systems. Apart from the island states, such as Cape Verde and the Comoros, only Swaziland and Lesotho bear any direct relationship to precolonial African states.

All of Africa's modern boundaries were the result of decisions taken in Europe between 1885 and 1900, with a few further adjustments after World War I as former German colonies were handed over to Britain, France, or Belgium. In other words, Africa was divided up according to the interests of competing European powers and with little or no regard for pre-existing African nationalities.

The result was twofold. First, boundary changes often resulted in the division of a single people between two different colonial powers. In West Africa, for example, a treaty between Britain and Germany in 1890 resulted in half of the Ewe people finding themselves under British rule in the colony of Gold Coast (now Ghana). The remaining Ewe initially came under German rule, and then in 1918 were transferred to the French. Similar divisions were to be found across almost every boundary in Africa.

We have been engaged in drawing lines upon maps where no white man's foot has ever trod; we have been giving away mountains and rivers and lakes to each other, hindered only by the small impediment that we never knew exactly where they were.

Lord Salisbury, English conservative politician and leader of the House of Lords (1925-1929) remembering the scramble for Africa.

HISTORIC RIVALRIES

There is a second problem arising from the arbitrary, colonial division of Africa. Within each African state there are now many different African peoples — some

After 14 years, the brutal Marxist dictatorship of Menguistu Haile Mariam came to an end in Ethiopia with the fall of the government palace to rebel soldiers on May 18, 1991. Here a rebel soldier wears a government officer's hat with the gold emblem removed.

of them historic rivals — who have little reason to trust each other. It is one of the most remarkable achievements of independent Africa that there have been so few civil wars over the past 35 years and that all but one of the continent's political boundaries have remained unchanged since 1960. The one exception has been Eritrea, which broke free from Ethiopia in 1993.

Most African governments have managed to hold their very diverse countries together with some degree of unity. However, lack of underlying trust and understanding between peoples of different regions has often seriously hindered the progress of development. Those in power have tended to favor the people of their own region. Consequently, funds for development projects have not always gone to the regions where the need has been greatest.

FROM DEMOCRACY TO DICTATORSHIP

When Britain and France withdrew from Africa, they appeared to leave modern democracies behind them. Within a few years, however, many of these democratic systems had collapsed, giving way to authoritarian one-party states or outright dictatorships. A number of these changes were the result of military coups.

Why did democratic structures dissolve so quickly into dictatorships? The problem was that the colonial powers had not encouraged the development of any democratic tradition during nearly a century of colonial dictatorship. They had allowed political parties to be formed only just before independence. These parties were rarely created on a truly national basis. This was due to the huge number of languages and cultures within each newly-independent African state. In almost every country, Africans had no common language. English or French, the languages of colonialism, could have been adopted. However, to be fluent in one of these languages required education, something that the colonial authorities had done little to promote.

At independence, most Africans were illiterate. Only a minority could speak English or French. To succeed, a politician had to speak in the language of the electorate. As a result, political parties almost always evolved around the old African ethnic and regional divisions. When every political party in a legislature represented a different region, there was little hope of a government achieving agreement on a national scale. Politicians argued that the multiparty system in Africa encouraged ethnic rivalries and divided the people rather than uniting them.

THE ONE-PARTY STATE

The party in power often sought to solve ethnic rivalry by declaring a one-party state. In other words, all opposition parties were banned. Any politician who wanted to run for a seat had to join the ruling party. In some one-party states an unpopular politician, or even a minister, could lose his seat at a national election. This occurred both in Zambia under Kenneth Kaunda and in Senegal under Léopold Senghor. However, the governments of most one-party states became very dictatorial and undemocratic.

The problems of Africa's multiethnic nation states were the political consequence of independence. After independence, African unity was fragile and the democracies were unstable. This has made it difficult for African countries to develop into prosperous and democratic modern states.

SUCCESSFUL DEMOCRACIES

Of all the African countries that gained independence during the 1950s and 1960s, Botswana and Mauritius stand out. These two states are the only two to have achieved an unbroken record of multiparty legislative democracy. Circumstances in Botswana could be seen as exceptional. The opposition parties were always very small and weak, and the governing political party was never seriously challenged in elections until 1994. Mauritius, on the other hand, encompasses huge ethnic differences. It showed great political maturity when the long-standing government was ousted in dramatic general elections on two occasions. Mauritius is an island state located in the Indian Ocean, however, and its situation cannot be expected to be typical of continental Africa.

THE CULTURAL LEGACY

The colonial legacies of language and religion have had both positive and negative effects upon independent Africa. English and French — the official languages of the government in most African countries — provide an element of impartiality in the face of potential ethnic or regional rivalry. However, the use of European languages in the education system has had a negative impact upon the evolution of distinctly African culture, philosophy, and thought.

The French Community of African Nations and the Commonwealth of former British colonies may provide a link between countries of the former French and British empires. In West Africa, however, the cultural legacy of the colonial period has had an adverse effect. The linguistic and cultural division between former English and French colonies has created a serious barrier, hampering the proper integration of the West African Economic Community, founded in 1976.

The texture of the policy thinking of a Houphouët-Boigny [of Ivory Coast] is simply not the same as that of a Nyerere [of Tanzania]; nor does Samora Machel of Mozambique view the world through the same prism as Daniel arap Moi of Kenya . . . More than rhetoric separates Brazzaville and Kinshasa, Dar es Salaam and Nairobi, Cotonou and Lagos. Even the most casual visitor to these contrasting capitals will sense the divergence.

C. Young, Ideology and Development in Africa, (Yale, 1982), page 10.

MILITARY POWER

Of Africa's 54 countries, 32 have experienced a military *coup d'état* at some stage in their independent history. Indeed, between 1963 and 1983 almost every change of government in Africa took place with a sudden, often violent overthrow of those in power.

The military coup of 1966 in Nigeria resulted in civil war (1967-1970). This was the first serious African attempt to change the international boundaries imposed by Europe. The Igbo people's struggle (seen here) to set up an independent "Republic of Biafra" was defeated by the Nigerian army in January 1970.

From 1963 onward, coup followed coup with frightening regularity. Ghana, for example, has suffered five coups and Nigeria no fewer than six. Why has the military been so prominent in African affairs? Has its role been a result of independence from colonial rule? To answer these questions one needs to look at the history of armies during the colonial period.

COLONIAL ARMIES

At the time of independence most African countries inherited standing armies from the departing colonial regimes. It is important to remember that Europeans conquered Africa at the end of the nineteenth century using armies made up largely of African soldiers. The officers were always European, but they recruited local Africans to make up the regular troops. These colonial armies were generally ethnically-based, and they were often greatly resented by the people that they had helped to conquer. Many colonial countries started life under military occupation. Once the initial conquest period was over, the primary purpose of the army was to help the government wield power over the people. Its role was to oppress and discipline civilians, not to fight against the professional armies of other countries. In addition to their lack of experience in professional combat, colonial soldiers were often poorly equipped. These were the kind of armies that most African countries inherited at independence.

The incoming civilian governments during the early 1960s viewed their new national armies with some trepidation. Army officers often demanded modern military equipment, as their price for supporting the government. Civilian politicians had other priorities. They preferred to spend government money on schools, housing, and health facilities.

During the colonial period African armies had served as a branch of government. Military force had been particularly useful for collecting taxes from a reluctant civilian population. Thus, when armies seized power in successive *coups d'état* during the 1960s and 1970s, they were simply reinvesting themselves with the role that they had served before independence. The leaders of many of the early military coups in Africa claimed that they were rescuing the people from corrupt and incompetent civilian governments. In reality, however, it was often the threat of a cut in the military budget that lay behind the timing of a coup.

CIVIL WAR

What is happening in Nigeria is not the problem of Nigeria alone. You can see it from the stupid mimicry that is taking place in Sierra Leone, in Gambia, where some wretched, miserable, empty-headed mutineers decided they had the right to take over the destiny of millions of people without any cabinet qualifications, any vision, nothing but the notion of power.

Wole Soyinka, Nobel prize-winning Nigerian writer, on his country's failure to democratize in the 1990s, quoted in the Guardian, *February 27, 1995.*

Only eleven of Africa's 54 countries have suffered protracted periods of civil war since independence. Considering the enormous ethnic mix of peoples within almost every one of Africa's states this is very surprising. In a large country like Nigeria, for instance, there are literally hundreds of different languages spoken, and there have been major historic and cultural divisions between the peoples of the north and those of the south. Levels of regional distrust reached such heights in the country that a civil war was fought between 1967-1970. Despite these great differences, Nigeria has managed to avoid civil war since 1970, and it remains one of the great dynamic forces of the continent.

In Sudan the British themselves had administered the colony as two separate entities until just before independence. The Arabic-speaking, Islamic north had little in common with the largely Christian African south. Indeed, in precolonial times, people from the north had often raided the south to hunt for ivory and to capture slaves. The divisions caused by culture, language, and religion in Sudan remained after independence. This has led to almost continual civil war as the north has sought to forcibly impose its rule, culture and religion on the south.

The war in Chad — fought throughout most of the 1970s and 1980s — was made worse by the direct interference of Libya, which for many years occupied the northern quarter of the country. As we have seen earlier in the book, the civil wars in Angola and Mozambique (see page 49) were also the result of interference by external powers.

Civil wars also broke out in Liberia and Somalia. These conflicts arose out of political power struggles and rival banditry that followed the collapse of corrupt and destructive military dictatorships. Somalia, awash with arms from both the Soviet Union and the U.S.,

Our objective [in crushing the Biafran rebellion] was . . . to maintain the territorial integrity of our nation, to assert the ability of the Black man to build a strong, progressive and prosperous modern nation, and to ensure respect, dignity and equality in the community of nations for our prosperity. . . . Long live one united Nigeria.

General Gowon, Nigerian Head of State, January 1970, quoted in Oliver and Atmore, Africa since 1800, (Third edition, Cambridge, 1981), page 338.

An eight-year-old boy holds his own on the streets of Monrovia, April 1996. Liberian ethnic rivalry erupted into civil war following the collapse of the military dictatorship of Samuel Doe in 1990. A West African peacekeeping force eventually established an interim government, and the rival leaders agreed to elections in May 1997.

had never had the chance to evolve a democratic tradition. The emergence of political parties between 1990 and 1991 quickly degenerated into open conflict between well-armed rival clans. Their only unity of purpose was in opposition to what they saw as "outside interference."

INDEPENDENCE IN UGANDA AND ZAIRE

Uganda's problems after independence stemmed from the ethnic makeup of its colonial army. The army was northern-based, and it was used to keep the northern dictators Milton Obote and Idi Amin, in power. A Tanzanian invasion helped remove Amin in 1979, but when Obote seized power again a group of Ugandan patriots began a guerrilla war of liberation. For five years during the early 1980s, they fought Obote's second regime and, in the process, built up a new national and non-ethnic army for the future. When they came to power in 1986, this National Resistance Movement was able to cast off the colonial past and set Uganda on a positive road of reconstruction and development.

In Zaire the main cause of civil conflict in the early 1960s was the chaotic rush to independence by the Belgian government. The oppressive colonial government had done much to isolate the people from the African nationalist movement sweeping the rest of the continent. The Belgians discouraged the development of any sense of nationhood, preferring to keep the various regions isolated from one another. When political parties were finally legalized in August 1959, no fewer than 120 emerged. Unscrupulous politicians whipped up regional and ethnic fervor among the long-oppressed and ill-informed electorate. With a constitution still not finalized, elections were held just weeks before independence in June 1960. Within days of the election, the army mutinied and the copper-rich province of Katanga (modern Shaba) declared its independence from the republic.

Into the chaos that followed the secession of Katanga, the United Nations (UN) first sent a peacekeeping force and then intervened, ending Katangan secession in 1963. Moise Tshombe, the Katangan leader, became prime minister of what was then known as Congo-Kinshasa. The UN withdrew in 1964, and almost immediately a major rebellion broke out, paralyzing the government for much of 1965.

General Mobutu's military *coup d'etat* in 1965 finally restored order to Zaire. However, his corrupt dictatorship, which persisted until his fall in 1997, did little to help the country overcome its potential for further internal conflict. (See page 71.)

BLOODSHED IN RWANDA

To some extent, the conflict in Rwanda can be traced back to colonial intervention. In precolonial times, Rwanda was governed under a sophisticated and highly centralized form of kingship. The peasant majority in the country were known as the Hutu and the aristocratic minority called themselves the Tutsi. These distinctions were not rigid matters of class or race. A Hutu who acquired cattle or distinguished himself in war could be accepted as part of the aristocratic Tutsi class.

When the Germans colonized Rwanda they believed that the Tutsi were a superior racial group — second only to the Europeans themselves. On the strength of this belief, they introduced identity passes, thus defining people once and for all as Tutsi or Hutu. The Tutsi were then educated and placed in positions of trust in the colonial civil service. The Hutu were left to live as

White mercenaries from South Africa and Rhodesia were employed by Moise Tshombe to help maintain his Katangan secession from the Congo. This picture, taken in January 1963, shows a group of them relaxing before withdrawing from Kolwezi in the face of advancing United Nations troops.

uneducated peasants, oppressed by demands for forced labor on government projects. Thus, what had, in pre-colonial times, been Hutu resentment of Tutsi central government became, under the far harsher regime of the colonial period, a deep-seated hatred of all ethnic Tutsi.

The Belgians took over from the Germans in 1919 and began to make moves toward independence in 1959. At this point the long-oppressed Hutus rose up in rebellion and massacred thousands of Tutsis. The children of the massacred Tutsis fled into exile in Uganda. A generation later they returned to overthrow the Hutu dictatorship in a war that lasted from 1990 to 1994. When the Tutsi-led Rwanda Patriotic Front was on the point of winning the war, the government's Hutu militias began a genocidal attack on all Tutsis in Rwanda, forcing them to flee *en masse* to Zaire.

Within weeks they had killed three-quarters of a million Tutsi, as well as many Hutu moderates. Before they could complete the genocide, however, the Rwanda Patriotic Front won the war, forcing the Hutu killers to flee to Zaire. They were accompanied by up to two million Hutu refugees who feared Tutsi revenge for the massacre.

As the Tutsi-led army of the Rwanda Patriotic Front advance on Butare, Rwandan Hutu refugees, implicated in the genocide of 700,000 Rwandan Tutsi, flee to Zaire under the protection of French troops, July 1994.

ECONOMIC CRISIS

At independence European colonial governments left Africa with a mounting economic crisis — the end product of three-quarters of a century of colonial misrule. Africa's economies had been directed toward providing Europe with cheap raw materials. In return, Africa imported relatively expensive manufactured goods, such as cars, trucks, machinery, tools, utensils, clothing, and even processed food, from Europe. Throughout the colonial period there had been little or no attempt to develop African economic self-sufficiency. The basis of Africa's economic problem is summed up in the words of a former Tanzanian Minister of Finance: "Africans produce what they do not consume, and consume what they do not produce."

TERMS OF TRADE

Even the "terms of trade" were determined outside Africa. The developed world of Europe and North America dictated the prices of Africa's raw material exports as well as the cost of Africa's manufactured imports. The "balance of trade" always remained firmly in Europe's favor. Africans had to produce larger cash crops and more minerals each year for export to the European market in order to import the same amount of manufactured goods. The situation was summarized by Ugandan President Yoweri Museveni who remarked in 1989: "In 1970 we needed 212 bags of coffee to buy a seven-ton Mercedes Benz truck. In 1987 we required 420 bags and now (in 1989) we require more than 530 bags to secure the same vehicle."

While more and more effort was put into cash-crop production and exploiting the mines, subsistence cultivation was neglected. Thus, by the early 1960s Africa, which had fed itself for thousands of years, had become a net importer of food.

In the early years of their independence, African governments invested very heavily in establishing the manufacturing industry. They believed that this would end their need to import all their manufactured goods. To do this, however, Africans had to import expertise, technology, machinery, and building materials from Europe or North America. As a result, their foreign debt mounted, and they had to produce even greater exports of cash crops and minerals in order to pay interest on their debts. Things got dramatically worse in the early 1970s as a serious recession hit the developed world. This meant that Africa was paid a lot less for its raw material exports.

ECONOMIC DISASTER IN ZAMBIA

As we have seen, many of Africa's economic problems were a consequence of its colonial past. They also stemmed, however, from mistakes made by Africa's

Kenneth Kaunda, President of Zambia 1964-1991. Although ultimately un-successful in his economic policies, Kaunda played a leading role in the 1970s and 1980s in international attempts to isolate the racist regimes of Rhodesia and South Africa. Here in 1986 he spoke out strongly against British Prime Minister Margaret Thatcher's reluctance to isolate South Africa.

early independence rulers. The case of Zambia illustrates this point. In the words of Zambia's former President, Kenneth Kaunda, the independent state of Zambia was born in 1964 "with a copper spoon in its mouth." Zambia was one of the world's largest producers of copper, and from the 1950s until the early 1970s the world price of copper was booming. Copper mining was the British colonial government's only interest in Zambia. As a result, copper accounted for 92 percent of Zambia's foreign earnings and 53 percent of total government income. Consequently, at the time of its independence Zambia had huge reserves of foreign exchange.

Kaunda's government spent lavishly on free education, health, and a whole range of prestigious building projects in the capital, Lusaka. Very little effort was made to develop other aspects of Zambia's economy. Crucially, there was no investment in farming and food production. The government developed a huge and expensive civil service and the rapid expansion of nontechnical education drew people away from the rural areas. They flocked to the cities where they believed that the government would give them jobs. Almost without realizing it, Zambia, a huge, fertile, formerly self-sufficient agricultural country, suddenly found that it was no longer able to feed itself. It had to import even the most basic of foodstuffs. Suddenly in 1973, as the developed world went into recession, the world price of copper collapsed, and Zambia received only half the former price for its copper exports. The Zambian economy went into a spiral of decline from which it has never really recovered.

MOUNTING NATIONAL DEBT

By the early 1980s, Africa's debts to the banks of the developed world were so large that many African governments were having to take out new loans in order to pay the interest on old ones. Since then the World Bank, based in Washington, has been making serious efforts to help African governments readjust their economies so they will be able to pay off their debts. To some extent these efforts are succeeding and most African governments are now paying the interest on their loans, but at a terrible price. In order to pay these debts, governments are having to drastically cut back their spending on education, health, and housing.

How can we depend upon gifts, loans and investments from foreign countries and foreign companies without endangering our independence? ... How can we depend upon foreign governments and companies for the major part of our development without giving to those governments and countries a great part of our freedom to act as we please? The truth is that we cannot.

Government of the Republic of Tanzania, 1967, pp10-11, quoted in Morag Bell, Contemporary Africa, (Longman, Harlow, 1986), page 120.

We are strong advocates of liberalizing global trade arrangements. But, as a small country, we must use every means at our disposal to demand fair and responsible trade, and to persuade the major trading powers not to ride rough-shod over such apparently insignificant economies as our own.

Sam Nujoma, President of Namibia, addressing the World Food Summit, Rome, November 1996, quoted in West Africa, November 25, 1996, page 1851.

The basic shortcoming of the World Bank's program in Africa is that it concentrates on the paying off of foreign debts rather than helping the continent become self-sufficient. This has led to a continuation of the old colonial pattern: concentration on cash crops for export at the expense of food crops for local consumption. The best agricultural land and expensive new irrigation schemes in countries such as Kenya and Zimbabwe have been set aside for the cultivation of crops for export.

In the sub-Saharan countries like Niger, Chad, and Burkina Faso, subsistence farmers have been pushed onto marginal lands previously only used for cattle and goats, while the grazing animals have been pushed to the margins of the desert. The results of this were illustrated in 1984, a year of severe drought in the countries bordering the Sahara. The cotton farmers of Niger produced bumper crops of cotton, while local food crops failed and herders lost up to 90 percent of their livestock. A small number of cotton farmers did quite well, and interest was paid to foreign banks, but the bulk of the population faced starvation.

Millions of dollars of Western aid is poured into Africa every year, but even this is not as much as Africa is paying out to the banks of the developed world. It is a vicious cycle from which there seems to be no escape for Africa.

In the countries bordering the Sahara, drought is a perennial problem, resulting in a high death toll among both humans and animals.

ASSESSING THE ACHIEVEMENTS

Some people wonder whether Africans might have been better off today if they had remained under European rule. It is always important, however, to recall the principal purpose of the European presence in Africa. It was certainly not intended to be for the benefit of Africa, although some Africans were able to pick up some benefits along the way.

In the final years of colonial rule, some constructive development work was done. However, this was largely because the colonial authorities knew that African self-rule was on the horizon. They realized that they were obliged to make preparations. If the colonists had believed that they would rule Africa until the end of the century, it is unlikely that even these limited projects would have been undertaken. The neglect and brutality displayed by later regimes in Rhodesia and South Africa serve as vivid illustrations of this point.

Africa has suffered many problems since independence in the 1960s. Some of these are the result of their colonial inheritance, and others are a consequence of African mistakes and misrule. The newspapers and television stations of Europe and America tend to focus on disasters for their news stories. This makes it very easy for outsiders to get the impression that Africa has achieved nothing positive. The image of the continent as a bankrupt, drought-stricken disaster area is very misleading. In fact, there has been a great deal of positive achievement in Africa since independence.

Looking back on the early decades of African independence, the historians of the future are likely to highlight its achievements at least as much as its failures. They will be able to contrast its levels of health and education, and its economic, social, and political development very favorably with the neglect, oppression, and exploitation of the previous hundred years.

One of the great achievements of African independence has been the massive expansion of education since the early 1960s. In the early 1950s barely 15 percent

People cannot be developed, they can only develop themselves. A man develops himself by joining in free discussion of a new venture and participating in the subsequent decision. He is not being developed if he is herded like an animal into a new venture.

Mwalimu Julius Nyerere, former President of Tanzania, speaking at the World Food Summit, Rome, November 1996, quoted in West Africa, *November 25, 1996, page 1850.*

These secondary school students in South Africa are benefiting from the ANC government's commitment to providing free education for all children.

of the population of tropical Africa were able to read and write. By the mid-1980s this figure had risen to more than 60 percent. In the late 1940s none of the French or Portuguese-speaking colonies of tropical Africa had a university. Even in the English-speaking colonies there were only a handful of colleges of higher education. By contrast, within 20 years of political independence there were hundreds of African universities. Many professionally-qualified African doctors, lawyers, and university academics were earning widespread respect for their work at home and abroad. In January 1997, the most senior position in the United Nations, that of Secretary General, was taken by Kofi Annan, a Ghanaian.

The vast expansion of modern health services has been another great achievement in Africa over recent decades. In 1960 an average of 40 percent of children were dying before the age of five. Within 20 years in many countries from Senegal and Ivory Coast to Tanzania and Botswana, this had been reduced to less than 20 percent, despite the fact that malaria kills up to two million Africans a year, most of them children.

POLITICAL CHANGE

There have been positive developments on the political front in recent years, too. The democracies inherited from colonial rule were very recent institutions and were not a true reflection of the inheritance of the colonial period. In most African countries there had been too little time to develop a culture of democracy and these European-imposed images of democracy were soon cast aside as inappropriate or unworkable. By the late 1980s, however, the political culture of Africa had changed.

Between 1989 and 1994 the political face of Africa underwent a dramatic transformation. There were many reasons for this. The most important external event to have a positive impact on Africa was the fall of the Berlin Wall in November 1989 and the subsequent ending of the Cold War. This meant that Africa was no longer the scene of Cold War rivalries. As a result, corrupt dictators could no longer rely on support from one or more of the superpowers simply because they declared themselves to be pro-East or pro-West. Almost immediately, the United States, Britain, and France — the main donors of aid to Africa — began to attach conditions to their contributions. Only administrations that could provide evidence of good governance were eligible for aid. This was usually taken by the aid donors to mean multiparty democracy.

CALLING THE DICTATORS TO ACCOUNT

For the first time in nearly 30 years, African dictators found themselves vulnerable to internal criticism. At the same time, the continent's economic problems were reaching crisis proportions, and the ordinary citizens of Africa were feeling in desperate need of some positive change in direction. Meanwhile, those Africans who had benefited from the great educational expansion of the 1960s were reaching their late forties and early fifties. They had lived all their adult lives in independent Africa and they had seen the failure of successive African governments.

This new generation of Africans had the education and experience to lead their countries in new directions. All over the continent, they decided that it was time to call their rulers to account. One after another,

After 27 years, one-party rule in Zambia by Kaunda's United National Independence Party (UNIP) came to an end with multiparty elections on November 1, 1991. Here a Zambian crowd, full of hope for the future, celebrates UNIP's electoral defeat.

African dictators were called — sometimes protesting — to the constitutional conference table. In some countries, like Zambia and Malawi, one-party constitutions were revised, and a change of government was achieved through the ballot box. In others, like Benin or Mali, the constitutional conference itself assumed the authority of government, redrafted the constitution, bypassed the incumbent head of state and conducted multiparty elections. In Seychelles and Ghana, rulers who had come to power by military *coups d'état* managed to supervise credible transformations to multiparty rule and get themselves elected as civilian heads of state. In Togo, Cameroon, Gabon, and Congo the quality of the elections were somewhat questionable, but even here critics were now much more willing to publicly voice their criticisms. Even in countries which have suffered recent *coups d'état* — Sierra Leone in 1992 and The Gambia in 1994 — the incoming military have protested their commitment to democracy. After a period of constitutional revision, they have in both cases returned their countries to civilian democracies in 1996. In Sierra Leone the incoming civilian government achieved the triumph of bringing a long-running, simmering civil war to a peaceful conclusion before the end of the year. In The Gambia, the military ruler managed to keep himself in power by resigning from the army before successfully competing for the civilian presidency in the democratic elections of 1996. In the second half of the 1990s, all of these new fledgling democracies encountered their first real test as democratically-elected rulers when they faced their electorates for the second time.

ZAIRE BECOMES THE "NEW" CONGO

In May of 1997, after Mobutu Sese Seko fell from power (see page 61), Zaire was renamed Democratic Republic of Congo, referred to here as "Congo." Congo's role in southern and central Africa, its mineral riches, the corrupt leadership of Mobutu — all led to the present situation with rebel leader Laurent Kabila taking over the country. Africa-watchers are hopeful, yet wary. There is much to be done to ensure Congo's leadership and solid economic footing. Several nearby countries, like Rwanda and Burundi, could benefit from Kabila being in power. Kabila was also supported by Angola and Uganda, for historical reasons that have been touched upon earlier here. Yet, depending

We solemnly honor the pledge we made to ourselves and to the world, that South Africa shall redeem herself and thereby widen the frontiers of human freedom . . . . We will redeem the faith which fired those whose blood drenched the soil of Sharpeville and elsewhere in our country and beyond.

Nelson Mandela, South Africa's first freely-elected President, on the occasion of his signing his country's new constitution, December 10, 1996, quoted in the Guardian, *December 11, 1996.*

This is a map of modern Africa. The entire continent has now achieved complete independence from the colonial powers of Europe.

on how well the "new" Congo stabilizes under Kabila's leadership, many countries could experience a negative effect, especially if this new government fails.

Some five million people in Congo supported the rebels. They had suffered long enough under Mobutu and his corrupt regime. This is surely a situation where the world must wait and see what the long-term outcome will be.

A POSITIVE OUTLOOK

On the economic front Africans in the 1990s are trying to find their own solutions to Africa's economic problems. For example, they are trying to achieve greater regional trade and economic cooperation. Provided there is increasing political stability on the continent, there is no reason why Africans should not be able once again to grow most of their own food, to develop their own industries, based upon the processing of their own raw materials, and to depend upon their African neighbors for their manufactured imports. In this way they would stand a chance of finally breaking free from the crippling circle of international indebtedness and aid, to achieve true independence at last.

GLOSSARY

African nationalism
The movement among Africans to achieve independence from colonialism.

ANC
African National Congress (South Africa).

apartheid
The South African system of laws that rigidly enforced racial segregation from 1948 to 1994.

assimilation
The system whereby the French encouraged a small number of educated Africans to reject their own culture and adopt the culture and language of France.

civil war
War fought between the people of one country.

colony
A country ruled by a foreign power, in which the citizens of the colony do not have equal rights with the colonizer.

conscription
Enlisting people into military service against their will; draft.

constitution
The system of laws and customs established and followed by a government.

coup d'état
Taking over the government of a country by force.

CPP
Convention People's Party (Ghana).

democracy
Government by the people or their elected representatives.

discrimination
When those in positions of power deny equal rights to others.

elite
A very small group of privileged or well-educated people.

Fascism
An absolute political system stressing the importance of nationalism and the country's leader.

FRELIMO
Frente de Libertação de Moçambique (Mozambique).

guerrilla war
Informal warfare by small groups, usually against a formal army.

migrant workers
People who regularly work for short periods away from home because there is no local work for them and no accommodation for their families where they work.

mining compound
Accommodation for migrant mine workers, usually fenced in and strictly controlled.

MPLA

Movimento Popular de Libertação de Angola.

palm oil

A vegetable oil crushed from the nuts of the tropical African palm tree.

racial segregation

A system giving people different rights, jobs, and places to live, according to their race or the color of their skin.

refugee

Someone who has had to flee from his or her homeland.

slave trade

The forcible transportation of millions of captives out of Africa for sale into slavery.

Socialism

The political system that stresses welfare and equality above individual profit.

subsistence cultivation

Small-scale farming that enables a family to grow just enough food to feed itself.

SWAPO

South-West Africa Peoples' Organization. South-West Africa is now called Namibia.

UDI

Unilateral Declaration of Independence (Rhodesia, 1965).

UGCC

United Gold Coast Convention. Gold Coast is now called Ghana.

UNITA

União Nacional para a Independência Total de Angola.

Western aid

A system whereby the well-developed, industrialized countries, mostly in Western Europe and North America, lend or give to the poorer countries of the world, many of which are African.

TIMELINE

1787 — Sierra Leone settlement founded by freed slaves from Britain.

1807 — Britain outlaws slave trading in British ships.

1822 — Liberia settlement founded by freed slaves from America.

1830 — French invade Algeria.

1861 — British annex Lagos Island (Nigeria).

1869 — Suez canal opens.

1870 — Diamond mining begins in Kimberley, South Africa.

1877 — British annex Boer republic of Transvaal (South Africa).
— H. M. Stanley completes navigation of Congo River.

1878 — Leopold II of Belgium sends Stanley to take control of Congo.

1879 — French begin railroad construction east from Dakar (Senegal).

1880-1881 — First Anglo-Boer War, Transvaal regains independence from Britain.

1882 — British annex Egypt.
— French annex Congo-Brazzaville.

1884-1885 — Berlin Africa Conference.

1884-1900 — European scramble for Africa.

1886 — Gold mining begins in Johannesburg, Transvaal (South Africa).

1888 — Swahili, Hehe, and Yao rebellions against Germans in Tanganyika.

1890 — Anglo-German and Anglo-Portuguese treaties settle many of the modern boundaries of Africa.
— British colonization of Rhodesia (Zimbabwe) begins.

1893 — French conquest of Tukulor Empire.

1895 — Mazrui Swahili rebellion against British in coastal Kenya.

1896 — Ethiopia defeats Italian invasion at battle of Adowa.
— Ndebele and Shona rebellions in Rhodesia.

1898 — French conquer Samori's Mandinka Empire (Guinea).

1899-1902 — Second Anglo-Boer War (South Africa).

1900 — French conquer Bornu (Chad).

1904-1908 — Nama and Herero rebellions in South West Africa (Namibia).

1905-1907 — Maji-Maji rebellion in Tanganyika.

1908 — Congo Free State becomes Belgian Congo.

1910 — Union of South Africa: Britain grants self-rule to whites in South Africa.

1912 — Founding of ANC in South Africa.

1914-1918 — World War I.

1915 — Chilembwe rebellion in Nyasaland (Malawi).

1919 — Former German colonies handed over to France, Britain, and Belgium.

1922 — Independence for Egypt.

1935-1936 — Italian invasion of Ethiopia.

1939-1945 — World War II.

1941 — Liberation of Ethiopia.
— Eritrea occupied by British.

1946 — French colonial reforms in West and Equatorial Africa.

1947 — Independence for India and Pakistan.

1951 — Independence for Libya.

1952 — British hand over Eritrea to Ethiopia.
— *Coup d'état* in Egypt.
— British declare state of emergency in Kenya.

1953 — British settlers form Central African Federation.

1954 — Nasser becomes President of Egypt.
— Fully-elected internal self-government in Gold Coast (Ghana).
— War for the liberation of Algeria begins.

1956 — Suez canal nationalized. British and French attempts to recapture canal defeated.
— Independence for Morocco, Tunisia, Sudan.
— Internal self-government in French West and Equatorial Africa.

1957 — Independence for Ghana.

1958 — French referendum in West and Equatorial Africa.
— Guinea votes "Yes" and becomes Independent.

1960 — Independence for French West and Equatorial Africa (Senegal, Mauritania, Mali, Niger, Chad, Ivory Coast, Burkina Faso, Togo, Benin, Cameroon, Central African Republic, Gabon, Congo-Brazzaville).
— Independence for Nigeria, Zaire, Somalia, Madagascar.
— Macmillan's "Wind of Change" speech in South Africa.
— Sharpeville massacre in South Africa.

1961 — Independence for Tanzania, Sierra Leone.

1962 — Independence for Algeria, Uganda, Burundi, Rwanda.

1963 — Independence for Kenya.
— Breakup of Central African Federation.

1964 — Independence for Zambia, Malawi.

1965 — Independence for The Gambia.
— UDI in Rhodesia (Zimbabwe).

1966 — Independence for Botswana, Lesotho.

1968 — Independence for Swaziland, Mauritius.

1974 — *Coup d'état* in Portugal.
— Independence for Guinea Bissau, Cape Verde.

1975 — Independence for Angola, Mozambique.

1976 — Independence for Seychelles, Comoros, Equatorial Guinea.
— Soweto uprising in South Africa.

1980 — Independence for Zimbabwe.

1985 — State of emergency in South Africa.

1988 — South African defeat in Angola.

1989 — Free elections in Namibia.
— Fall of Berlin Wall, end of Cold War.

1990 — Independence for Namibia.
— ANC and other political parties legalized in South Africa,
— Nelson Mandela released from prison, constitutional negotiations begin in South Africa.

1990-1994 — widespread multiparty elections in Africa.

1993 — Independence for Eritrea.

1994 — Free elections in South Africa, Mandela becomes President.
— Genocide in Rwanda.

1996 — Mandela signs new constitution for South Africa.

1997 — Civil war in Zaire and fall of Mobutu; name changed to Congo.

FURTHER READING

Bentley, Judith. *Archbishop Tutu of South Africa.* Enslow, 1988.

Bigelow, William. *Strangers in Their Own Country*, "A Curriculum Guide on South Africa." Africa World, 1987

Bond, George, series editor. *Heritage Library of African Peoples*, 56-vol. series. Rosen, 1994-1995

Bradley, Catherine. *Causes and Consequences of the End of Apartheid.* Raintree Steck-Vaughn, 1996

Brynes, Ron. *Exploring the Developing World: Life in Africa and Latin America.* University of Denver Center for Teaching, International Relations Publications, 1993

Clark, Leon E. *Through African Eyes, Vol. 2: The Present, Tradition and Change.* Center for International Training and Education, 1994

Glickman, H. (ed.) *Ethnic Conflict and Democratization in Africa.* African Studies Association Press, Atlanta, 1995

Harris, Sarah. *Timeline: South Africa*, "Weighing Up the Evidence" series. Trafalgar, 1988

Hoobler, Dorothy and Thomas. *African Portraits*, "Images Across the Ages" series. Raintree Steck-Vaughn, 1992

Jones, Constance. *Africa, 1500-1900*, "World History Library" series. Facts on File, 1993

Meyer, Carolyn. *Voices of South Africa: Growing Up in a Troubled Land.* HarBrace, 1986

Middleton, Nick. *Southern Africa*, "Country Fact Files" series. Raintree Steck-Vaughn, 1995

Otfinoski, Steven. *Nelson Mandela: The Fight Against Apartheid.* Millbrook Press, 1992

Smith, Chris. *Conflict in Southern Africa*, "Conflicts" series. Simon and Schuster Children's, 1993

Winner, David. *Desmond Tutu*, "People Who Have Helped the World" series. Morehouse, 1990

Worth, Richard. *Robert Mugabe — Zimbabwe*, "In Focus Biographies" series. Silver Burdett Press, 1990

Zimmermann, Robert. *The Gambia.* Childrens Press, 1994

INDEX

ACKNOWLEDGMENTS

The publishers are grateful to the following for
permission to reproduce photographs:

Cover photo (large): Corbis-Bettmann
Cover photo (small): The Mary Evans Picture
                        Library
Corbis-Bettmann: pages 9, 20, 22, 23, 25, 28, 31,
32, 34, 35, 41, 43, 51, 52, 54, 62, 64, 70; The Mary
Evans Picture Library: pages 8, 10, 13, 14, 15, 18,
19, 27, 30, 38; Hulton Getty: pages 17, 29, 48;
Hutchison: pages 6, 66, 68; Popperfoto: pages 24,
35, 44, 46, 49, 57, 59, 61.